MW01124081

E-mails
from

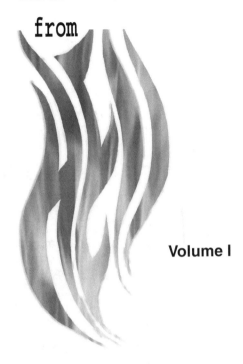

Volume I

The Wrath of William Wyndell

A collection of obnoxious and
rude e-mails presented by

David M. Earthman

Houston, Texas
2005

ISBN# 0-9763386-0-2

www.EmailsfromHell.com

Project Coordinator — Rita Mills
Cover Design — Bill Megenhardt
Illustrations — Bill Megenhardt
Text Design — Rita Mills
Editor — Anderson Bracht

Disclaimer: All conversations in *"E-mails From Hell, Volume 1: The Wrath of William Wyndell"* are real. However, all names, addresses, phone numbers, and e-mail addresses have been changed to protect people's privacy rights. Any similarities are completely coincidental. The name 'William Wyndell' is fictitious and is the portrayed character. Any name similarities are completely coincidental.

Some conversations have been edited for readability.

The paper used in this publication meets the requirements of the American National Standard for Permanence of Paper for Printed Library Materials Z39.48-1984.

Printed in the United States of America

E-mails from Hell

Table of Contents

E-mails

from

CHAPTER ONE

On Death

Dear Andersell Funeral Home.

I am sending this e-mail in an attempt to gain some information that will ease my mother's worries.

She is weeks from death and we are beginning to talk about arrangements. But she has an issue which I don't know how to answer. Hopefully you can help me.

She is concerned about the embalming process. Her concern, as is mine, is about the pain she will endure while being embalmed. I have assured her that it is probably painless, as you guys have probably done the procedure hundreds of times. Could you tell me a little more about what she should expect?

After we have discussed our options, I would like to come see you to make the final arrangements. I will await your response with further details.

Sincerely, William Wyndell

Reply: Advance Planning Associates . . .

Mr. Wyndell,

Thank you for requesting information regarding the final arrangements for your mother. As for your question regarding embalming, there will be no feeling of pain because the embalming process takes place after death has occurred. She has nothing to worry about.

As far as sitting down and making those final arrangements, I will be more than happy to do that with you at your convenience. If you have any additional questions regarding the embalming process, feel free to call our funeral home to speak to a licensed funeral director. Again, thank you for your interest in Andersell Funeral Homes.

Jim Kelchner — Advance Planning Associate

To: Garden Funeral Services
From: William Wyndell
Subject: *Mounting Question*

Dear Sir or Ma'am:

I am sending this e-mail with the saddest of hearts. I would greatly appreciate some feedback on some questions I have about your funeral services.

I have a loved one who is near death and we are making arrangements for that final day. It won't be much longer. The loved one I am talking about is my father, who loved hunting his entire life. His living room is filled with mounts of various wild game, such as deer, bass, birds, elk, etc. It is my father's last wish to have his body preserved and mounted.

We can't make up our mind whether to half-mount him for a spot above the fireplace, or mount him in such a way that it looks as if he is standing, holding his gun, and about to take a shot. I am not sure whether to deliver the body to you, or do we need to take him to a taxidermist?

Whichever, I do have a few questions before we bring you the body:

1. Once he is mounted and stuffed, how long will he be safely preserved in our living room?

2. Will hot or cold weather have any effect on the preserving?

3. How much will it cost…do we pay by the pound or the limb?

4. Is there any lingering odor or smell we should be aware of?

I am sorry for so many questions, but I know very little about your industry. I will look forward to your reply. Perhaps we can set up a meeting and discuss this further.

Warmest regards, William Wyndell

Reply: Garden Funeral Services . . .

Mr. Wyndell.

I have received your e-mail, but am unable to help you. It is illegal for human remains to be stuffed and kept at home. However, I might be able to offer you an option. There is a company, www.memorialartist.com, that will take the cremated remains of an individual and incorporate them into a painting. For example, you could have your father cremated and then have a picture of him painted in the pose that you described to me in your e-mail. This company would use his ashes in the paint and that would allow you to have a part of your father with you always. I really have no other options to offer in a legal sense or suitable to your needs. Best of luck.

Sincerely yours, Glenn E. Milkey, Director

Reply: William Wyndell . . .

Dear Mr. Milkey,

Thank you for the information that I requested. I have relayed
the message that we cannot stuff or mount our father to my
siblings. The painting idea sounds like an option. I have
actually heard of that before. Do you have any idea how much
that costs? I am also unfamiliar with the cremation process.
Does it hurt?

Should we decide to cremate our father, are there other options that we could do with the remains? For instance, my sister asked if we could put the remains in one of those balls that you shake and it looks like it is snowing inside. Would that work or would the ashes just turn to mud?

Or, could we use the ashes in another art form? Perhaps mixing it with clay and making a ceramic vase or coffee pot is a possibility?

I appreciate your feedback and advice. We will consider all options and make a decision very soon. You have already been a great service to our family in this time of need.

Sincerely, William Wyndell

Reply: Garden Funeral Services . . .

Hi Mr. Wyndell,

There are a few options available with cremation. You probably cannot put the remains in a snow glow, but you could have them added to clay and make some kind of pot. You could also purchase a nice urn and make a display at your home. There are some nice hunter urns, for example.

The cremation process itself is a simple procedure whereby the body of an individual is returned to the elements more rapidly than through burial. It does not hurt because once cellular death occurs, there is no feeling in the human body whatsoever.

Hope this helps.

Sincerely yours, Glenn

CHAPTER TWO

On Marriage

Hello. I would like to speak to you about the wedding dress you are selling. My fiancée is very interested in it. Well actually, I just ordered a wife from one of those Filipina bride order sites. She will be here in about 3 weeks. I would like to show up at the airport with the dress in hand so we can go straight to the chapel.

Do you have any other accessories you can throw in? Why are you selling it? Talk to you later.

William Wyndell

Reply: Letty Reyam . . .

Hi! Thank you for answering my ad.

Well, the dress is in perfect condition. We can meet so you can see the dress. I have the bouquet, diadem, and lace. I even believe I have the little groom and bride for the cake! The dress is $350 and $30 for the bouquet, diadem and lace. You can call me if you want to meet. I'm in Austin. My telephone number is 555-8473. Where are you? I've been e-mailing another person who is also very interested in the wedding set. Naturally, whoever comes first with the money, will get the dress.

Take care, Letty

Reply: William Wyndell . . .

Hey Letty. How are you? Wow, that sounds great, and I would appreciate that little groom and bride for the cake. Do you think you could color the bride to make her look Filipina?

Also, I am not sure the exact size of my bride because I haven't met her yet. I think she is supposed to be average size. I am just PRAYING that they send me one with a nice rack and nice ass.

I live in Round Rock, so I am close. I want to see it. What about any sexy wedding underwear or garter belts…do you have any that I can buy or where should I go to get that stuff? Talk with you soon. Have a great day.

William

Reply: Letty Reyam . . .

Hi William!

Sorry that I didn't get back to you sooner. I wanted to look for all the wedding items I have before I e-mailed you. And another reason is that I talked to somebody before I talked to you. This person is very interested in the wedding set…the problem is that he's in Africa!

We were making arrangements for payment and shipping. I told him that I will sell it to whoever comes first with the money. He told me that I'll receive the check tomorrow (Friday). I guess I'm going to wait just one more day. If I don't get it by then, you can come over and see it on Saturday or Sunday, and see how many other things I have. He didn't ask me for anything but the bride's attire, so the wedding night-clothes are completely for you.

You were asking me about sexy wedding underwear and garter belts. I have a pair of sexy, never-worn wedding panties that you will love and a sexy negligee for the wedding night! Sorry, I don't have a garter belt.

I don't have school tomorrow, so I'll have time in the evening to look for more items that you might need. Do you know her sizes? I might have the shoes. Please let me know if you want to meet Saturday or Sunday afternoon. I live in South Austin. My telephone number is 555-8473.

I really think the way you want to receive your bride at the airport is sooo nice!! Ahhh!! She will be very happy to meet you, especially with everything set up for her. Good luck!!

Take care, Letty

Reply: William Wyndell . . .

Hello Letty…how are you? Well, let me know what the African says and if he makes good on his promise to send the check. If not, I would love to see the dress as early as Monday.

As far as the sexy attire…is the underwear edible? I probably won't be interested in the negligee or any kind of nightie. As far as I am concerned, she is going to be butt-ass naked for the first 4 days. Are you a teacher or something? Me too.

William

Reply: Letty Reyam . . .

Hi William. No, I am not a teacher. I am taking tax classes, and I'm working full time. I'm still learning English. Spanish is my first language. Where do you teach?

Tomorrow I am going to be busy, but I'll have some time around 1-2 P.M. I have to be ready for the KISS & Aerosmith concert after that!! Is Saturday OK with you?

Ciao, Letty

Reply: William Wyndell . . .

Hi Letty. Obviously last weekend wasn't good for me or I would've e-mailed you sooner. I went to the concert, too. Man, I would love to see Steven Tyler and Gene Simmons get into a fistfight.

Anyway, the good news is I finally saw a picture of my fiancée. You can rest easy because they are sending me one with a really huge rack. I don't know about her mud-flaps, but if they are too big, I'll put her on a strenuous exercise regimen starting immediately.

So things are looking good. She will be here very soon. Did that African send the money for the dress yet?

William

Reply: Letty Reyam . . .

Hola William. I was on the first row at the concert. It was great. I got a rose from Peter Chris!! I love Paul Stanley...he still looks very good.

Well, that guy told me he was busy with his father-in-law's funeral. I don't want to wait anymore. So if you want to meet, I'll be available Tuesday after 6:30 P.M. Please let me know if that works for you.

Letty

Reply: William Wyndell . . .

I can't do it Tuesday night. I have to see my Parole Officer.

Then I have to go to my Narcotics Anonymous meeting. What other day is good for you?

Reply: Letty Reyam . . .

I could make it Friday night. I have a test tomorrow night, and class on Thursday. Friday or Saturday is OK for me, obviously I'll have more time on Saturday. What day is better for you?

Letty

Reply: William Wyndell . . .

Well Letty, to tell you the truth, I have to spend the weekend in lock-up. This is the last weekend I am to serve of my sentence and I need to finish it before my mail-order bride gets here.

Reply: Letty Reyam . . .

Do you have to be there on Friday or Saturday? If you have time Friday, I'll have time for you. I have class on Monday, Thursday and a test on Wednesday. Are you going to be available next weekend?

When is your bride coming over? I'm sorry about your week-end. Be sure and take many books with you. My reading recommendation for the altar: 1 Corinthians 13.

Take care, Letty

Reply: William Wyndell . . .

I already told you that this weekend isn't good. I will be doing my best to keep from getting poked while I'm in the pokie.

Next week might be better.

My bride is coming the following week. I hope she cooks good because I ain't got shit to eat around here. What in the world is 1 Corinthians13? Is that some sort of secret code for something?

William

Reply: Letty Reyam . . .

Do you still want to do business?

Letty

Reply: William Wyndell . . .

Hi. Sorry it has taken me so long to get back with you. Well, they sent Phong Duk over here, but unfortunately her rack wasn't as big as I wanted. So she is on her way back to the Philippines.

The good news is they are going to send me a fresh new one in about 10 more days. If you have other offers, then go ahead and sell the thing. If not, we can talk when they send the next potential bride over. Oh yeah, I really like that Corinthians passage. But aren't there supposed to be like snakes and serpents that eat everybody?

William

Reply: Letty Reyam . . .

You are going to need a dress sooner or later. With your busy schedule and mine, we should try to meet, and that may happen in a week. I honestly believe that my dress is going to fit her perfectly. I'm sure she is going to be kind of petite, with big breasts and big hips. I'm 5'4".

The ad is going to run in the Chronicle again tomorrow, so if you still want to meet, let me know.

Letty

Reply: William Wyndell . . .

You got a point. So is the dress fit for a broad with a big chest and big hips?

Reply: Letty Reyam . . .

The (front) top has a beautiful veil cleavage. The (back) top has a cleavage with some pearl lines, and this makes it more beautiful and elegant. The (back) bottom is open, so the bride can "show" her legs every time she walks. Yes, it is very sexy!

The train can be removed for the after-wedding festivities. I believe the dress will fit sizes from 5-9.

Letty

Reply: William Wyndell . . .

Hey Letty. Well, I don't want a dress that is going to show everyone her beaver or mud-flaps. Would we be able to sew it together to hide those areas? I don't mind people seeing her rack…that's fine. Maybe next week is best for me. How about you?

Reply: Letty Reyam . . .

The dress is sexy, but decent. Friday after 6 P.M., or Saturday after 11 A.M. is OK for me.

To:	redheadcool@hotmail.com
From:	William Wyndell
Subject:	*Diamond Ring*

Hi. I would like to talk to you about the diamond engagement ring you are selling for $400. You say it was never worn? Why not? You must've gotten dumped, huh? Well, don't worry about it, toots. You'll find love again.

$400 is pretty cheap…and you say it has diamonds on it? I bet I got pimples on my back that are bigger than the diamonds on that ring…but I am still interested. Let me know what we need to do to make this transaction.

Thank you, William Wyndell

Reply: Misty Muir . . .

Actually, ASSHOLE, I did the dumping. If you have pimples on your back bigger than my ring, you have problems.

I wouldn't sell my ring to a jerk like you.

Misty S. Muir

Reply: William Wyndell . . .

Good morning, Misty. I don't want us to get off on the wrong foot. Now look here, sweet cakes, I would still like the ring, even AFTER you insulted my dermatological problems. So in conclusion, do we have a deal, honey melons?

William

Reply: Misty Muir . . .

I told you I will not sell my ring to you. You insulted me first. Don't you even feel sorry for people who have to cancel their weddings? Do this…imagine your future fiancée in the position of calling off her own wedding and then having to sell her ring. As if that wasn't bad enough, some asshole e-mails her and says, "So you got dumped, huh?". Anymore light?

Misty S. Muir

Reply: William Wyndell . . .

Good morning, Misty.

Now listen up, sweet cakes. I am a simple guy and I enjoy the simple things in life, like lollipops and hot butter in my ass. I am sorry you had to dump your fiancé. He probably deserved it…am I right or am I right? Now back to the issue at hand…how about that ring, honey-baby? Hurry back.

William

To:	lisa_macha@harts.com
From:	William Wyndell
Subject:	*I Want Your Wedding Dress*

Hi there.

I am interested in the wedding dress you are selling. My fiancée and I are getting married soon and finding a cheap dress has been a first class pain in the ass.

So your dress is only $250 and you advertise it has never been worn? What happened…did he leave you or something? I am a guy and am not quite sure about the whole size thing. Your dress is a size 24? I don't think she is THAT fat…she's pretty fat, but maybe fat like a size 20 or so. Will your dress be way to big for her? If not, I will tell her to start eating before the wedding. As far as I am concerned, the fatter the woman the better. Nothing worse than a skinny woman…am I right or am I right?

So, please let me know what I have to do to take that dress off of your hands.

Regards, William Wyndell

Reply: Lisa_Macha@harts.com . . .

Well, first…wedding dresses go according to sizes that were around in the 1930's and 1940's. The dress will fit her fine. And if she is smaller, it will give her room for alterations. Yes, I am asking $250…and I just want to get it off of my hands. The tags are still attached and it has a bag. It is very beautiful for a very beautiful woman, which I imagine your fiancée is. A picture of the dress is attached. Please e-mail me if you are definitely interested in it. Thank you.

Lisa

Reply: William Wyndell . . .

Dear Lisa,

Thanks for sending the picture of the wedding dress. You are right…it is indeed beautiful. But I am not sure what you are saying about the sizes. Guys use that same sort of rhetoric when they have small penises. They say, "it's not he size of the ship, but rather the motion in the ocean", and all girls will tell you that is a bunch of BS. Am I right or am I right?

So it looks like I will probably take it. I will show "Piggy" the picture you sent and if she loves it like I do, then it's a done deal. You never answered my question…did you get left at the altar or something? This dress isn't hot is it?

How about accessories and stuff like that? I imagine if you and she are about the same size, you must have some fat feet, too. What size hooves do you have, and do you have any shoes we can buy? How about jewelry?

Please advise and hurry back. William

Reply: Lisa_Macha@harts.com . . .

Okay, first off…I want to sell you the dress…but you really have to start taking into consideration peoples' feelings. No, I do not have "fat" feet, and they aren't hooves. Some of the things you have said have offended me a little. You are marrying the woman for a reason, right? And as for the reason why I am selling the dress, well, it is irrelevant to the situation at hand.

But now if you are not interested in the dress, then I would understand. But I was offended by your comments towards me

and definitely towards your fiancée. And as far as being "hot/
stolen", no, I paid over $700 for it.

Thank you. Lisa Macha

Reply: William Wyndell . . .

Hello Lisa. Now listen here, honey cakes, I didn't mean to
offend you at all, so get your panties out of a wad. I can choose
to call my fiancée whatever I want, because I love her. Same
reason why I hit her…it's because I love her. Besides, she knows
when I hit her I am doing it out of love, not anger or hate.

We would still like that dress. Do you have any bridesmaid
dresses?

William

CHAPTER THREE

On School Enrollment

To:	Darsky@stanthony.org
From:	William Wyndell
Subject:	*School Enrollment*

Dear Mrs. Darsky:

My name is William Wyndell and I am new to the Houston area. My family and I recently moved here from upstate.

I would like to enroll my child in your school next year, but I have a concern or two that I would like to share with you.

My son, Bill Jr., has a rare disease that makes his skin smell after he begins to perspire. Exposure to sunlight, physical activity, or temperature changes brings out the sweat, and it doesn't take much to get it going. It is an incredibly awful smell…similar to that of body odor mixed with raw sewage. In the past, some parents have complained, and Bill Jr. has had other students tease him, call him names, and harass him to the point of wetting himself in front of the class.

We now have a plastic bubble-type sphere which has it's own thermostat control. We were able to use it last year at Bill's school and had great results. Would it be possible for Bill to bring his bubble to school should he be accepted for admission? We would be happy to make a contribution to your school, in line with any problems you may foresee.

I will look forward to your response.

Regards, William Wyndell

Reply: Megan Darsky . . .

Dear Mr. Wyndell,

Billy sounds like a very courageous young man. I would be glad to have you stop by and visit our campus and see if we might be a right fit for your family. You did not mention what grade your child is applying for. We will need his grades and the appropriate test scores to begin the application process. Please contact the admissions office and they will send you an application packet.

God bless you in your search for a school for your son.

Thank you, Mrs. Megan Darsky

Reply: William Wyndell . . .

Dear Mrs. Darsky.

I appreciate your reply and your sincerity. Yes, Billy is a very courageous young man. We love him just like a house pet.

In response to your questions, he is currently being home-schooled. As I said, we just moved down from the panhandle of Texas. In response to your 2nd question, Billy is in 3rd grade. He is 12 years old. I know that he is older than most kids in his grade, but this is merely the result of all the enrollment problems we've faced at his previous schools. Let me assure you that he is in no way mentally impaired or mentally slow.

I can send his transcripts if you still don't foresee any problems with our situation. I love the campus. I attended church there on Sunday and took a gander at the facilities. It will be perfect. I will wait for further instructions.

Sincerely, William Wyndell

Reply: Megan Darsky . . .

Dear Mr. Wyndell,

I find it truly offensive that you compared your child to a house pet. If you are going to make statements like that, our school will not meet your needs. Your child will be in my prayers.

Mrs. Darsky

CHAPTER FOUR

On Learning Foreign Languages

To:	portufred@hotmail.com
From:	William Wyndell
Subject:	*Learning Portuguese*

Hello. I read your ad and understand that you teach Portuguese. I am taking a trip to Brazil in December and need to learn the language. The only things I know are "konichiwa" and "kompai"! How much are your lessons and when can I start?

Another question...is it important that I allow my chest hair to grow out before I go to Brazil? I understand Brazilian women love a nice hairy chest on a man. Shouldn't be a problem if that's the case. I can look like Chewbacca in about 2 months if need be. Please advise with answers and further details.

Thanks and adios.

William Wyndell

Reply: Frederico Saillios Gebores . . .

Hello there, William. Thanks for the message. As far as the chest hair, I think just a little will do. A good sense of humor, though, is imperative to conquer the hearts of tropical women, and judging from your e-mail, I think you are on the right path. As far as classes, I am confident that I can get you ready for pick up lines in Portuguese in no time.

As far as costs, I have developed a six-week course for a total of $130.00 (materials included). Are you free either Mondays or Wednesdays after 6 P.M.? I teach at the Grant School, which is located at 61st street, between Red River and Duval. Do you speak any Spanish? Do you have access to a VCR?

Let me know about your schedule. We can start as early as Monday, July 14th. If you have any other friends who might be interested in having fun learning a new language, be sure and let them know as well.

Obrigado e Ate logo. (Thanks and see you soon.)

Frederico

Reply: William Wyndell . . .

Hey, thanks for the reply. I do not speak any Spanish (other than "get outta my way, you Mexican" when I am driving across town in traffic). I do have a friend who might be interested in your class, however,

I don't think I can do those days though. Monday is BINGO night, and Wednesday nights are usually spent shampooing the gerbils…then catching a late movie.

Yes, I have a VCR…also have quite a nice porn collection… but that's beside the point. What else can we work out?

Hurry back.

William

P.S . . . tell me how hot the chicks are in Brazil

Reply: Frederico Saillios Gebores . . .

Thanks for the message and sorry for the delay…I was out-of-town yesterday. Since Mondays don't work for you, below I have outlined some times I have open in my schedule. It would be great to have another student meeting with us during those times for conversation sake, but regardless, you'll be exposed to lots of Portuguese and Brazilian culture. By the way, Brazilian chicks are hotter than anything I can describe. You'll have to check it out for yourself and tell me later.

Evenings are best for me. Friday's and Saturday's are tricky because I play music and do lots of traveling on weekends, playing original Brazilian and Latin American music. I hope you can find an hour in your schedule that'll match mine. Let me know. Peace. Frederico

Reply: William Wyndell . . .

Alrighty…now look here, Pancho…I don't care about your travels and really could care less about your dumb band. I just want to learn Brazilianese so I can talk to all the hot babes.

So, evenings will work for me. I, too, work in the daytime…I tune pianos part-time and sing karaoke the other part-time. Let me know when you want to meet. Is Brazilianese hard to learn?

William

Reply: Frederico Saillios Gebores . . .

I'll see you next Monday, July 14th @ 6 P.M. I'll be expecting you at the Grant School. Please bring $130.00 to cover your initial 6 classes and materials. Also, bring a notebook and a pen. I highly recommend that you purchase a Portuguese-English dictionary.

See you Monday. Frederico

Reply: William Wyndell . . .

You must have some sort of Brazilian tuba shoved up your ass and it's blocking air to your peanut brain. What part of "Monday is BINGO night" didn't you understand? Try again, Pancho, and hurry back. Last time you made me wait too long. Also, you never answered…is Brazilianese going to be hard to learn?

Take care. William

Reply: Frederico Saillios Gebores . . .

You'll have to learn Portuguese somewhere else. I don't take students who are insulting. Goodbye and good luck.

Frederico

To:	elsagig1@austin.rr.com
From:	William Wyndell
Subject:	*Italian Lessons*

Hi there. My name is William and I would like to talk to you about learning to speak Italian. I think it is a beautiful language. I am intending on traveling there in a few months and the only thing I know in Italian is "Mama-Mia, Papa-Pia, baby's got the diarrhea". Can you help me out?

How much will lessons cost and when can I start? Also, maybe we could have a language exchange? I have lived all over the world, so if you need help, I am fluent in American English, Australian English, and British English.

Ciao. William Wyndell

Reply: Elsa Gigoli . . .

Ciao William,

Thank you for your interest in 'Lessons from Italy' language classes. We meet every Monday from 7:00-8:00 P.M. at my place. The total price is $195.00 and the balance is due in advance. Certificates of completion are available. NO refunds on missed classes. Let me know if you are interested and are in!! — Elsa

Reply: William Wyndell . . .

Hey Elsa, thanks for the reply. Mondays are no good for me. I have my Narcotics Anonymous meeting, followed by AA, then followed by my Anger Management Class. So as you can see that day is super busy. Do you offer it on any other days?

Please let me know. Thanks. William

Reply: Elsa Gigoli . . .

What about a Tuesday @ 6:00 P.M. class? Each class is 1 hour long. Let me know your intentions.

Elsa

Reply: William Wyndell . . .

Tuesday night is kickboxing night. Thursday, Saturday and Sunday I have to do court appointed community service for the next 3 years. How about Wednesday?

Reply: Elsa Gigoli . . .

I am sorry, but Wednesday's are kind of full for me. Right now the only opening I have is Tuesday afternoon. Regarding your exchange deal, I will pass. Maybe my English is not perfect, but I need to pay bills…and feed my kids.

I will let you know when I have the next class.

Grazie, Elsa

CHAPTER FIVE

On Sales

To:	dianamc@aol.com
From:	William Wyndell
Subject:	*Vitamin Sales*

Hello Diana,

I am inquiring about the sales position you are seeking to fill. But, before I can start, I must know what it is I am going to be selling.

I can assure you that you won't have another worker like me...I'm the best. I know we are in a bear market, but these jerks need to buy, buy, buy. Am I right or am I right?

I also understand you will only employ me on a part-time basis. That is perfect because if you hired me full-time, I probably wouldn't work as hard and would slack off for half of the time.

So in conclusion, I will take the job. All I need from you now is the starting date, pay, benefits, and what the hell it is I am to sell. Then you can leave the rest to me. Am I right or am I right?

I look forward to hearing from you.

Kindest regards, William Wyndell

Reply: dianamc@aol.com . . .

My phone number is 555-2789. Will you call me so we can meet this week? I would love to tell you all about the business. The product is vitamins, and the company pays commissions each month as you help build the business. I assume you go to UT?

You will be hired by Frank Lima Marketing. I am a recruiter for them, and I am looking for people who will work the business. I will train you on how to work the business. This company works like a membership in which you sponsor 3 people to become members and take the vitamins each month. They in turn also help to sponsor three more people to help build the business, and so on.

Reply: William Wyndell . . .

Dear new job personnel:

No, I don't go to UT. I have already received my degree from Our Lady of the Brown Water in Harlingen, Texas.

Now look...I told you in my first e-mail that I will take the job. What I don't understand is all this vitamin sales lingo. What is a "puppy dog" sale? Will I be selling animals, too? Don't I need some sort of animal permit to do that?

So...do you want me to sell those vitamins (and dogs) or what? I am ready to start. Won't you answer my questions as best you can so I can get the show on the road.

Thanks so much. William Wyndell

Reply: dianamc@aol.com . . .

I would like to meet with you Wednesday late afternoon or early evening so I can tell you more about the business. If you want to add success and prosperity to your life, then this is the business for you. I have to meet with you first to get you started. I have to find out whether you are willing to buy the vitamins for yourself before you sell them. If you aren't willing to buy the vitamins, you won't be able to sell them.

I joined the program because I want success and prosperity in my life and I am willing to tell others like you about the vitamin program so the business will grow. I won't be home today, but you can call me Wednesday at my house or I will be glad to call you if you give me your phone number.

Diana

P.S. There are no puppies, by the way. "Puppy dog" marketing is a concept I will explain to you when we meet.

Reply: William Wyndell . . .

Hello again Diana.

I would like to meet with you, too. I would definitely buy the vitamins for myself, if nothing else so I can have nice neon-colored piss. But that is just a bonus, and beside the point.

It will be no problem getting people to work under me to sell these stupid vitamins to other people. I am a sales guy...you got it, I'll sell it. Give me a freakin' box of dirt and I'll sell it to somebody.

So in conclusion, it looks like I am a "GO". I got the people, soon I'll have those god-damned vitamins, and I got the sales drive needed to succeed in this business. Tell me where to meet you and when, and I'll be there.

Hurry back. One more thing...should I call you "boss" now?

Regards, William

Reply: dianamc@aol.com . . .

Is there a way I can call you or you can call me at 555-2789? I like your motivation, which is a great contributor to success in this business. I can meet you Thursday evening at Kirby Lane Café on S. Lamar around 7 P.M. if you like.

Diana

Reply: William Wyndell . . .

Hey, what's up there boss? How the hell are ya? No, you cannot call me. You can never call me…are we clear? I think I can meet you at Kirby Lane Café…I know where it is. I got totally shit-faced there one night and beat up my waiter. Then I punched a waitress in the face that tried to break it up. What time do you want to meet?

Hurry back, William

Reply: dianamc@aol.com . . .

I don't like the way you are writing to me in this e-mail and I don't believe that you are professional enough for a business such as this. I won't be at Kirby Lane Café tomorrow night. Please don't write me any more e-mails, and forget that I asked you for your phone number… I wouldn't want to call you anyway. You have an obnoxious attitude, and I don't care to meet you.

Diana

Reply: William Wyndell . . .

So what are you saying? You don't want to be my "boss" anymore?

Reply: dianamc@aol.com . . .

I won't be your boss, and I won't "sponsor" you into the vitamin business. You aren't professional enough for this business.

Diana

Reply: William Wyndell . . .

Not professional enough? What are you talking about? You haven't even seen me put my sales skills to use. You could ask my old boss. The only reason I am not there now is because he and I didn't see eye-to-eye on certain issues and we got into a fistfight. Then he was saying something like "you are the best salesman I have ever had, but you are a jerk", or something like that…I don't know. I wasn't really paying attention. I was busy kicking his ass. Point is, I'll sell loads of those stupid vitamins. What do you say, boss?

William

Reply: dianamc@aol.com . . .

The job isn't about selling vitamins, but creating a down line of people who will buy the vitamins each month and tell their friends about it. I don't like you calling the vitamins "stupid". Do you take vitamins? Are you employed right now? You need to invest $120 of your own money to start in the business. If you don't have $120 to get started, then this isn't the business for you.

Diana

Reply: William Wyndell . . .

Hey there boss. Like I said, no problem. Of course I have $120 to get started. And yes, I do work, and yes, I do eat Flintstone vitamins (simply for the delicious taste).

It looks like we are back in business and I am again working for you. So, do I need to send you the $120 and you'll send me those god-damned vitamins or how do I get started? Hurry up and get back with me.

Reply: dianamc@aol.com . . .

I don't like your language, plus you refuse to call me and meet with me. I'm pasting my application to this e-mail. You can paste it to your word program and send it in listing me as your sponsor. You can send a $120 money order. The address is on the application.

You will need to sponsor one person within 5 weeks after you send in your application. Your commissions are paid from creating a down line of 243 people from your first 3 people, and you receive commissions on sales each month.

But listen…I don't really think you are serious or you would at least want to call me. I know you are just being an "ass".

Diana

Reply: William Wyndell . . .

Hey there. Top of the morning to ya, stupid. Did you have a good 4ᵗʰ of July weekend? Now look here...I made it clear a while ago that you CANNOT call me. You can NEVER call me...NEVER. I feel like I am repeating myself; I said I am still interested in selling those stupid vitamins, didn't I? I am going to get a money order and send it in soon. I will say that I was hand-picked by YOU to sell. I assume I can throw your name around over there if I need to get shit taken care of?

Alrighty then, boss, I'm looking forward to my new career selling this crap.

William

Reply: dianamc@aol.com . . .

Are you going to send in the application form I sent you? I don't really want to call you, as you are the "rudest" person I have ever e-mailed, and I "hate" rude people!!! I'll be surprised if you can sponsor even 3 people in this program with your negative attitude.

Reply: William Wyndell . . .

Hey there, boss. Sorry for the delay. I was away for the week-end. Went down to Boystown, Mexico to watch the "donkey show" and get shit-canned with a few of my beer buddies.

Now look...calling me names is no way to treat your em-ployee. And RUDE? What the hell are you talking about? I have never said one rude thing to you. You don't know me well enough to call me that.
I am sending the money order this week. And yes, I understand

the "sponsorship" deal...I get 3 people, they get 3 people, and so on. It is like that hair shampoo commercial with that hot-ass chick and she says "and they tell 2 friends, and so on, and so on". Am I right or am I right? What else do I need to know?

Hurry back. William

Reply: dianamc@aol.com . . .

I am not your boss!!!!!!!!!!!!!

To:	jswart01@email.com
From:	William Wyndell
Subject:	*Sales Position*

Hello Ms. Swartzen.

I saw your ad and see you are looking for a salesperson for your health and marketing company. I know I am your man.

Let's cut to the chase. I am not going to try to swoon you with a really killer resume with a bunch of hoo-ha on it, and I'm not going to tell you how great you are in business. I went to a crappy college and I don't care about getting rejected when making a sale. I am a CHAMP in front of people and have been a successful salesman for nearly 8 years. I have sold everything from tractor/trailers to non-existent health insurance policies to the elder. I will sell tons of whatever it is you have at your company.

So, now I will need the start date and the location of our

company. Then you can leave the rest to me. I am happy to be part of the team. You will not regret this.

Sincerely, William Wyndell

Reply: Jamie Swartzen . . .

Mr. Wyndell,

I appreciate your response. Jamie is sick and out of the office, so I am taking her calls and e-mails. I would like to see a resume and have some more contact information from you. Your sales background seems impressive and I would like to see your work history.

I am curious as to your comment on selling "non-existent health insurance policies to the elderly." I would like to know what you meant by that. We are looking for ethical sales people here. Our products are state of the art and high quality. We pride ourselves on the integrity of our products and expect the same level of integrity from our representatives. We are looking for honest people who can believe in our company's mission and can ethically execute their duties to better our consumers.

Thanks, Ralph Clark—Extra Enterprises

Reply: William Wyndell . . .

Good morning, Mr. Clark.

Thank you for the compliment. I must agree that my sales experience is impressive, indeed. As far as selling non-existent health coverage to the elderly, let's just say I left that job because I was in disagreement with my god-damned boss about what I was selling. I found that what I was doing was extremely unethical. I am an honest person and a person of morals. He was pressing that I sell the same policy to retards. When I refused...well...that was the end of that job.

That is one reason I feel so strongly that I am a perfect fit with your company. I believe in it and in our product, whatever it is. With that said, let's get going on this. I will be there on Monday morning, 9:45 A.M. sharp. I will be dress-ready so you can send me out into the field THAT afternoon. See you then, Mr. Clark.

Regards, William Wyndell

Reply: Jamie Swartzen . . .

Mr. William Wyndell,

I've heard a lot about you from my colleagues!!! I received your e-mail and I'm quite impressed with your sense of humor. I do hope ethics are a concern for you, due to the fact that I'm intrigued by your flare. I would love to meet with you. However, 9:45 A.M. on Monday will not be conducive to my schedule. Call me at 555-3585, so we can chat ahead of time!

Have a great day. I look forward to your call!

Sincerely, Jamie Swartzen—Sales/Marketing

Reply: William Wyndell . . .

Good morning, Ms. Swartzen.

Thank you for your response, and I am glad that your colleagues are impressed with my experience. Are you sure that you can't do 9:45 A.M. on Monday? I can't do it anytime Monday afternoon. Nickelodeon is having a "Matlock" marathon, so I will be preoccupied. So either you will need to reschedule your other appointment, or just count on my starting Tuesday at 8:30 A.M.

Thanks for really making me feel like part of the team. It is nice to feel welcomed. As far as whatever it is I do there, will I be required to do any heavy lifting? What is my sales area? And what is my per diem for gasoline? So…everything is looking great. I will see you on Tuesday morning. Have a super weekend.

Regards, William Wyndell

Reply: Jamie Swartzen . . .

William, William, William,

What are you thinking? Your priorities are way out of line!! "Matlock" is not on Nickelodeon!! Make sure you get your programs right!!! Well, I guess I should just rearrange my entire schedule to fit your television time slots!!! Monday at 8:30 it is then, William!!! Bright and early, and don't be late!!! By the way, since you are now part of the team, we have a little tradition that the new guy brings breakfast for the first week till he proves his/her abilities!!! Bagels or breakfast tacos for ten please!!! Look forward to meeting you!!

Sincerely, Jamie Swartzen

Reply: William Wyndell . . .

Good morning, Ms. Swartzen (or is it Mrs.?).

My mistake. The "Matlock" Marathon is on TNT. Nickelodeon doesn't have the quality programming that TNT has.

Now listen up, and listen good. I told you I would be there at 8:30 A.M. on Tuesday, not Monday. Another thing, I don't eat breakfast...never did. You probably shouldn't either. I don't like Sweet-n-Low, either. However, I will bring breakfast for the first week. Is there a bagel or taco shop near our office? Where is our office anyway, and what do I do there? Also, do I work only on commission, or do I receive a salary plus commission?

Looking forward to seeing you.

Warm regards, William Wyndell

Reply: Jamie Swartzen . . .

Mr. Wyndell,

Good Morning. I hope you had a lovely Easter. As we discussed, you DID say Monday. However, due to the fact that your sense of humor enlightens me, I will make a concession on your behalf and reschedule you for Tuesday at 12:45 P.M. As far as pay goes, I don't like to over-promise and under-deliver. We haven't met yet, and even though you seem to be sharp and witty, I don't know if this is something that you would be good at. Fair enough? However, your compensation will surprise even you!!

By the way...TNT was always a favorite of mine over Nickel-odeon. No offense!! Well, Mr. Wyndell, tomorrow it is then. I'm sure you're not the type of person that would set an appointment and not show up, so I look forward to meeting with you for approximately an hour tomorrow. The physical address: 621 Richmond Ave., Houston, Texas 77057. Please don't be late as my time is as precious as is yours!! Have a great day!

Best Regards, Jamie Swartzen—Sales/Marketing

Reply: William Wyndell . . .

Ms. Swartzen.

I did not have a lovely Easter. I don't believe in Easter...never did. For the last time, you listen, and you listen good. First you said to be there at 8:30 A.M., and now you are telling me to be there at 12:45 P.M. I can't do both. I was there at 7:30 A.M., but nobody came out. I feel like I have been given the run-around by you again. So far I have proved to be a good and loyal employee, yes? Do you treat all the rest of my co-workers like this? I have stated numerous times that I am the right guy for you because I feel so strongly in what we sell and our company. And speaking of that, what is the name of our company? Our company is a proven entity and our products are unsurpassed by any other. So with that said, let's try again.

Let me know what your schedule is and I will try to work around it. But if I am unable to do so, you will need to change yours again. Have a super day.

Warm regards, William Wyndell

Reply: Jamie Swartzen . . .

Mr. Wyndell,

Obviously, you are not very diligent at keeping up with your e-mails. I never said for you to be here at 8:30. I'm starting to think that what we have to offer is not something you would be good at.

I'm sorry you didn't have a good Easter. Seems to me you are not a very happy person. I hope you find what your looking for, but for now I've decided not to waste anymore time responding to someone who obviously doesn't have what it takes to be successful with our company. Have a great day. I hope the sun will shine on you today!!

Best Regards, Jamie Swartzen

Reply: William Wyndell . . .

Hello Ms. Swartzen.

Yes, you did say 8:30 A.M. on Monday. Can we just get past all of that? I am tired of playing "he said/she said" with you. I DO have what it takes to be successful at our company. You will see. Plus, I strongly believe in our products, so much so that I will buy a bunch of whatever it is for me.

One more note. I am a very happy person. You can ask my Mom. With that said, let's get this ball rolling. Hurry back.

Have a wonderful day. William

To:	recruiting@mattresses.com
From:	William Wyndell
Subject:	*Mattress Sales*

Hello. I would like to speak to you about the mattress sales position you are seeking to fill. I have several years of sales experience in the mattress industry.

I recently worked for a major furniture outlet store selling mattresses, but I was let go because I let a potential client's child jump around on the mattresses. That is not a big deal in itself, but after I showed the boy how to do a front flip, the parents were not too happy and told my boss. I can assure you that this will not happen again. I am good at selling mattresses…you'll see.

When would be the best time for us to get together to discuss this further? I am available for work immediately. I look forward to hearing from you with further instructions.

Sincerely, William Wyndell

Reply: Steve Janeman . . .

William,

After I stopped laughing, I realized that you probably won't be teaching any acrobatics to future customers, but I think I do like your style and your honesty. All I need is for you to contact me with or without a resume (of course a resume is always appreciated) and tell me what side of town you are in and we can begin to discuss your new career with Mattresses, Inc.

My contact information is below and I look forward to speaking with you.

Thanks William, Steve

Reply: William Wyndell . . .

Hi, Steve.

How are you doing? Yes, I know that story is crazy and I guess now that I think back, it is pretty funny. I also taught that same kid how to do a stomach-to-back tabletop trick on the bed. I don't really see the need to send you a resume. We both know I am your man.

I am pretty flexible about a location to start working. I live on the west side of town with my wife, but I also have a small apartment that I keep near the Galleria area…that's where I bring all my other chicks. So I can pretty much work anywhere that you need me. You will just have to let me know.

What is the pay and what are the benefits with this job? Do employees get discounts on mattresses? I am in need of a couple of new ones for my Galleria area place.

Looking forward to hearing from you.

William Wyndell

Reply: Steve Janeman . . .

William, I will be honest with you. Your comments took me off guard and we run a very professional work place. If you are seriously interested in speaking with us about a great career in the mattress industry, please call me at the office number below.

Steven Janeman

Reply: William Wyndell . . .

Hi! Great, and thanks! I accept the job. All I need to know is which part of town you want me to work, and whether I am an A.M. or P.M. shift employee. I'll be there. Let me know.

To:	topprints@swbell.net
From:	William Wyndell
Subject:	*Custom Printing Sales*

Hello. I would like to speak with you about the sales position you are advertising for. I understand you do custom printing apparel. I have done that for several years. I was recently working at Kinko's, but unfortunately I let my girlfriend take a Xerox of her tits and the print was left in the machine. My boss didn't have a sense of humor about it, so here I am talking to you. Some people have no sense of humor…am I right or am I right?

When would you like me to start?

Sincerely, William Wyndell

Reply: Clayton Spanding . . .

At least you are honest about why you left Kinko's. Did you do any outside sales? Send me your resume. If your background fits, I will be happy to talk to you.

Reply: William Wyndell . . .

Hi, and thanks for the reply. First of all, I wouldn't say I exactly "left" Kinko's...it was more like I was "thrown out" of Kinko's.

Secondly, I have many years of outside sales experience. I have sold everything from pork chops and meat, to doing B2B sales for an online brokerage firm in Houston. I can assure you sales is in my blood. Let's get together and talk further. What do you say? Looking forward to hearing from you.

Sincerely, William

Reply: Clayton Spanding . . .

William, let's talk. I am out of the office all day today and Monday. Please call me Tuesday and we can set a time to meet. My office is in the Clear Lake area. Where are you? I look forward to hearing from you on Tuesday.

Reply: William Wyndell . . .

I would love to get together. I know where Clear Lake is. I live in central Houston, near the Galleria. I don't have a phone right now. I was making my ding-a-ling girlfriend cut the yard the other day and she dropped the phone and ran over it with the mower. I have told her time and time again "hey stupid, DO NOT carry the phone with you when you do the yard work". Some people never listen...am I right or am I right?

Just tell me when you want me to come see you. It will not be a problem. Take care.

William

Reply: Clayton Spanding . . .

I will be in this afternoon or tomorrow afternoon. Either of those days works for you? I will be away from e-mail for the next few hours. You can call my cell at 832-555-7318 to schedule.

Reply: William Wyndell . . .

Can't do it today or tomorrow. I ordered a little Vietnamese baby from one of those magazines, and it's coming in this weekend. So I have to spend the week at the immigration office doing paperwork. How does sometime in the middle of next week sound?

Reply: Clayton Spanding . . .

William, I filled my open position yesterday. I appreciate your interest and will keep you in mind if I have another opening.

Thanks

To:	isa@legalmark.com
From:	William Wyndell
Subject:	*Legal Mark Sales Job*

Dear Mr. Mush.

I saw your advertisement for the Sales position at Legal Mark. Although I am currently employed, I am intrigued by your ad. Let's cut to the chase.

Your ad says, "I dare you to see if you measure up" to our sales standards. Well I am daring YOU to hire me. Are you familiar with the band KISS and their motto "YOU WANT THE BEST, YOU GOT THE BEST"? Well here I am. I am not talking about all this popcorn fart sales bullshit that most companies offer. I am talking about real selling and huge money. If your ad promises what it says, then I am your guy. I don't want to waste your time anymore than I want you to waste mine. The market is going up my friend and these assholes need to buy, buy, buy…am I right or am I right?

So, if you are tired of weeding out and going through worthless resume after resume, then let me know where and when we can talk. If not interested, no problem. When I change jobs, I'll be more than happy to work for one of your competitors. Talk with you then, boss.

Sincerely, William Wyndell

Reply: Gwen Magoris . . .

Hi. I received your resume regarding the Independent Sales Agent position with Legal Mark. In order to screen candidates most efficiently, I'm sending you more detailed information about the job before scheduling a phone conversation.

If you'd like to be considered for a position, please e-mail me to set up a phone interview. Feel free to call me with any questions. If you're not interested, there's no need to reply to this e-mail, and I wish you the best with your career.

Best regards, Gwen Magoris — Staffing Manager

Reply: William Wyndell . . .

Hello, Ms. Magoris.

Thank you for the reply. I am still interested in speaking to you about the sales position. I am flexible about where you want me to work. I can move to any of the cities you listed, or I could start right here in Houston.

I have several law contacts. I would say I have pretty good knowledge of the law, seeing as I was a security officer for seven years while attending college.

I find it hard to believe that you received my resume, seeing as I didn't send one. I told you from the onset that there was no need to play the resume game. I am overly qualified, extremely eager to start, and hungry to make the sale. With that said, we can even skip the phone "interview". I am sure you will like me, be impressed with me, and hire me, so what's the sense?

I guess Mr. Mush is taking me up on my "dare" to hire me. That is great. I like this company's attitude.

So when would you like to meet? I will await your response to arrange further communication. Thank you so much, Gwen.

Sincerely. William Wyndell

Reply: Gwen Magoris . . .

William,

Obviously that was a canned response to many who applied. I do like your gumption, but a phone interview is part of the process. Either call me or e-mail your phone number so we can get started.

You do understand that if you are hired, you will be required to attend a 1 week-long intensive training course in San Francisco?

Thanks, Gwen Magoris

Reply: William Wyndell . . .

Ok, we can do the phone interview. I figured it would be a waste of time, but hey, it's your dollar. Just give me a number and we can set it up for next Monday. Also, I will call collect, so make sure to answer the phone.

Yes, I am aware that after I am hired I will have to come to San Francisco for a week of training. That is okay with me. Maybe if we hurry and do this, I can catch a Giants playoff game. Is it a possibility to get some tickets through the company, perhaps as a hiring bonus? If not, I am sure there will be plenty of bars I can go get liquored up in and watch the Giants win the series. I will check for your response tomorrow.

Regards, William Wyndell

Reply: CB de Lios . . .

Hi William,

If you can send me your contact information and resume, we will try to set up a phone interview as soon as possible. Sorry for the delay.

Regards, C.B de Lios — Recruiter

Reply: William Wyndell . . .

Hi CB. I was already in contact with Ms. Magoris and we were planning a phone interview, but I never heard back from her. I assumed she decided against it and was ready to hire me. I was hoping to start during the playoffs. Now I guess I will have to settle for a 49'ers game. Do they still have that guy on their team...you know...that one guy that made that play?

When would be the best time for us to get this ball rolling? I am ready to start and put my sales skills to use.

William Wyndell

Reply: CB de Lios . . .

I'm taking over the recruiting. I will not be in the office today, but will be in tomorrow. Send me your contact information so I can call you and let's get the ball rolling.

CB

Reply: William Wyndell . . .

Okay great. What you are saying is that I should call and reserve a flight to San Francisco so I can come and fill out all my employment forms and receive training? What day do you need me there?

Also, will I need a heavy coat? It is still warm here in Texas, so if it is to be cold, please advise. Thanks so much.

Reply: CB de Lios . . .

Mr. Wyndell,

First things first. I need a copy of your resume and contact information so we can chat. Then if we decide to move to the next process, I will schedule a phone interview with one of our Sales Directors. After that, logistical planning can be discussed.

CB

Reply: William Wyndell . . .

Hello, Mr. de Lios.

Well, it's too late. I already bought a non-refundable ticket to San Francisco. I am coming in next Thursday. I think my plane arrives at about 11:30 A.M. Should we have the interview that day or the next? Are you sending someone to the airport to pick me up?

Reply: CB de Lios . . .

Mr. Wyndell,

We will not be there to pick you up...you do not work here...you will not be hired to work here, ever. Good luck.

Regards.

CHAPTER SIX

On Living, Rommates, and Rent

Greetings you.

I would like some information on the high-rise units you are selling at the Commerce Towers. I am interested in a single unit, but it needs to be large enough for me to have big and loud parties. Do you have something at the top or on an end?

Secondly, I raise cats. I currently have 48 cats living in my 1 bedroom house. I use a baby pool for the cat-box. So I will need a unit that has a window large enough for me to pour the kitty litter out. Again, I think the higher the better...that way by the time it hits the ground and/or people walking around down there, the cat shit will be scattered fairly well.

Please get back to me as soon as you can and let me know your thoughts. Thanks in advance.

William Wyndell

Reply: Stephanie Shandon . . .

Dear William,

Thank you for your interest in Commerce Towers. First, we have sound attenuation within our walls, which should prevent most noise traveling to neighboring condominiums. We do have two party rooms, which may be used for various get togethers.

Second, we have a pet policy at Commerce Towers, which prohibits the raising of animals within the premises. Residents are restricted to no more than 2 dogs, cats, or other household pets. Also we do no allow any materials to be thrown from our windows, as this is a hazard to pedestrians below.

I wish you the best of luck in your search for a home that suits your needs. Good luck with all of your cats!

Kindest regards, Stephanie Shandon

To:	dan@handyjobs.com
From:	William Wyndell
Subject:	*Handy Man Job*

Hello Dan. I read your ad and understand that you are somewhat of a handyman. I have a job for you. We are decorating my daughter's bedroom with "candy-corn". She loves it. We want to glue the candy corn in rows so that it covers the entire room. Then when she gets hungry in the middle of the night, she can just bite one off, or lick it, or whatever youngsters do nowadays.

How much would you charge to come over and glue the candy corn to the wall? Would it be by the square foot or by each candy corn that you paste? Let me know.

Regards, William Wyndell

Reply: Dan Norton . . .

William, I do not believe this request will be a problem. Call me @ 555-3131 to make an appointment and I will be more than happy to come over and take a look at the job.

Thanks, Dan Norton — Dillo Construction

The Wrath of William Wyndell **61**

Reply: William Wyndell . . .

Hello Mr. Dan,

Thank you for the reply. I am glad we can do business. I was
hoping to gain a ballpark estimate. I measured the room. It is
10' x 9' x 9'. I already have 23 bags, each containing 20 lbs. of
candy-corn. We want it covered from top to bottom.

You can certainly do the job by yourself. However, this might
be a job that would require 2 people. Are there any other
employees over there at Dildo Construction?

Regards, William

Reply: Dan Norton . . .

I e-mailed you a few days ago. You can contact me @ 555-3131.

Dan — Dillo Construction

Reply: William Wyndell . . .

Hi, Dan. How's it going? Our phone is out of order because of
all the construction going on here. Plus, I don't know you well
enough to call you yet. So what are your thoughts?

William

Reply: Dan Norton . . .

This sounds like one of my friends playing a joke on me. My
rate is $35 an hour.

Reply: William Wyndell . . .

I can assure you that I don't know you. How many hours will it take you to complete the room?

Regards, William

Reply: Dan Norton . . .

Until I can see the job, I will not bid it. — Dan

Reply: William Wyndell . . .

I do not understand all this wishy-washy behavior and take offense to getting the "run-around" from you. Now look, son, I am not sure what kind of operation you are running over there at Dildo Construction Company, but if you are not the person in charge of operations, I would like to speak with someone who CAN get this job done for me. We need to do it this week. Thank you.

William

Reply: Dan Norton . . .

Mr. Wyndell,

I feel that I have been upfront with you. I do not bid a job until I see it, and I don't make a deal until I meet in person. That is my policy. When you are ready to move forward, you can contact me @ 555-3131.

Thanks, Dan Norton — Dillo Construction

Reply: William Wyndell . . .

Hello again, Mr. Norton, and thank you for such a timely response. I thought that I was clear in that I can't call you because I don't know you. That said, do you expect me to let a complete stranger into my house to look around? I already told you the configuration of the room, so what's the problem? Let's move on this.

I would expect to pay anywhere up to $2000. Now, if it will take 2 persons from Dildo Construction to do it, then it would be $1000 per person. The job should take a maximum of 2-3 days. So are we a go? Let me know, son.

Warm regards, William Wyndell

Reply: Dan Norton . . .

William, I am willing to go 2 people for 2-3 days for $2000.00, and $250.00 per day for each additional day.

Dan

Reply: William Wyndell . . .

Dan,

You will be finished with the room in probably 1 day, 2 max, and that's only if you and that other worker from Dildo Construction are slackers and spend your time being horses-asses.

So, talk to your friend and let's set up a time for you to start. When is good for you?

William

Reply: Dan Norton . . .

William,

First, it is Dillo Construction. I do take offense to any 'slacker' reference or having poor work ethics. I am a builder and a handyman. If you say the job can get done in one to two days, great. Then you will not have any problem with the agreement. If the terms are not agreeable, you will need to find somebody else.

Dan

Reply: William Wyndell . . .

Dan,

Thanks for the clarification. I was wondering why you decided to name your company Dildo Construction. Anyway, I still want you to paste the candy. But, I am wondering how you can assume it might take you a few additional days to do the job when you haven't even bothered to come out here and look at it first?

William

Reply: Dan Norton . . .

If you recall, you did not want me to come out and bid the job. I already offered.

Reply: William Wyndell . . .

I don't remember it that way. I remember giving you my phone number, and I even remember inviting you to come see the job, and if need be, have dinner with me and my family.

Reply: Dan Norton . . .

Sir,

You should go and read the previous e-mails that are on this page. You stated you did not want to invite a complete stranger out to your house and would not even give me your phone number. Please stop wasting my time.

Dan

Reply: William Wyndell . . .

Dear You:

I am beginning to wonder if you get ANY business at all after the way you give everybody the runaround. Now look here, son, if you want to paste these god-damned candies on our wall, we would still love to have you. I'll even have my wife cook up a meatloaf and we can celebrate over a cold can of Olympia.

I know you have my number and address because I gave it to you. Quit being a horses-ass. Quit being a slacker and under-achiever. Let's get this job rolling. Have a super day.

William

Hi. I would like to speak with you about the roommate ad you placed. I live and work off of 59...where are you located? I will be a good roommate. I do not have loud parties and I AL-WAYS pay my bills on time.

I must say that I do smoke...not that much at all...maybe just 34 cigarettes a day. Is smoking in the house okay, or will I need to go outside? Let me know.

Hurry back. William Wyndell

Reply: collector1@aol.com...

That is a pack-and-a-half a day, or 10 packs per week...

Reply: William Wyndell...

I know. See, I told you I wasn't a heavy smoker. So do you want to meet and talk about the roommate situation?

William

Reply: collector1@aol.com...

That is a lot of smoking, and about $150 a month. I would recommend that you stop and protect your health, and at the same time that money can be put towards your own apartment. Good Luck.

Reply: William Wyndell . . .

$150 per month? Gosh, I wish it were that cheap. So do you want me to use that money towards paying rent over there at your place?

Reply: collector1@aol.com . . .

Okay…call me on the phone and let's chat. Although, originally I wanted a female or a transgendered person.

Reply: William Wyndell . . .

Okay, what is your number? And what does transgendered mean? You mean one of those people that have both a penis and vagina? Or do you mean a gay dude that dresses like a woman? Please advise.

Reply: collector1@aol.com . . .

You are discusting! I think you need to go back to school and learn how to express yourself. I am not interested and do not bother me anymore.

Reply: William Wyndell . . .

Fine…I think you should go back to school and learn how to spell.

To:	shm33@swbell.net
From:	William Wyndell
Subject:	*Duplex for Rent*

Hello. I would like to talk to you about renting the duplex in Garden Oaks. $1000 sounds like a steal. I have an issue. I have a boat, and I was wondering if it was ok to park it either in the driveway or on the front lawn? The boat isn't that big…maybe 33'…so it will be hardly noticeable.

Thanks so much. William Wyndell

Reply: Sharlene Morrison . . .

I talked to the owner and he said to show and measure. There is a parking spot in the back property and he said to measure the width and (length 33').

Let's schedule an appointment for you to come see the inside and check out the parking situation.

Sharlene — 555-8141

Do you have any pets? How many occupants? What is your move date?

Reply: William Wyndell . . .

Hey, Sharlene…thanks for the reply. Well, I would probably need to park the boat in the front yard because I have one of those blow-up Moonwalk things (the kind you jump around in), and I was planning on putting that in the back yard. When I come home from work I like to drink beer and then jump around in it. But if it's okay to switch them and put the boat in the back and the Moonwalk in the front, then that is totally alright with me.

Also, there will be only 1 occupant, yours truly, and I have no pets to speak of. I can move in anytime. What is the next step?

Thanks, William

Reply: Sharlene Morrison . . .

Moonwalk? How big is it? Jump around in it? Okay, I'm sold. I want one (sounds fun). The front of the house would be your area. There should be room for your Moonwalk somewhere in your half of the duplex. There is a lot of yard space in your area. Did you measure the width of the boat? Bring all the measurements with you (boat and Moonwalk) and we'll see if they fit. Have you thought about boat storage? There is a place in the neighborhood.

What are your current rental obligations? Have you turned in notice at your current place? Where are you currently living? Garden Oaks? What are your work hours?

Sharlene, 555-8141

Reply: William Wyndell . . .

Hey Sharlene, how are you doing today? The width of my boat is only 15', so it's about 33'x15'. It should fit in the yard. I really don't want to put it in storage because I like to work on the engine really late at night. Seems when I am revving the engine in a storage unit, it gets smoky and I can't see anything. The Moonwalk is regulation size. Maybe I could work something out with the other neighbor about putting it in the driveway, or if the ceilings inside the house are big enough, I could put it in there.

I don't need to give notice where I currently live. I live in a sort of commune or cult house just outside of Garden Oaks, so I am free to move whenever I want. I work days until about 6 P.M. or so. I can't do viewing today…how about early next week?

William

Reply: Sharlene Morrison . . .

"The boat is out of the question. The civic association will not allow it"…quote from the owner. He was waiting to hear back from them.

If I find anything else I'll let you know, but at this point, I can't help you. Sorry.

CHAPTER SEVEN

On Music

To:	caldwell@yahoo.com
From:	William Wyndell
Subject:	*Drummer*

Hey man…are you looking for a bad ass drummer for your band?
Look no further…I am it. I play a double bass drum with 9 toms
and 10 cymbals. Not only can I jam, I sometimes light my body
on fire when I do my drum solo. How does that grab ya?

I last played in a Death/Speed metal band, but I can play
fuckin' anything. When do you want me to start? Let me know
more information about your band.

Rock on, asshole. William

Reply: Caldwell Haine . . .

Hi, William. Thanks for your interest. Judging from your e-mail,
I'm probably not your can of Red Bull. You can listen to some
basic demos for four of my songs at www.caldwellmus.com.

My style is more adult groove with some jazz, funk, folk, and
maybe some country sounds to it. I suspect my music would
put you to sleep if you feed off of speed metal. It still amazes
me how some speed metal drummers can play fast while
keeping excellent timing.

I'm looking for a groovin', laid-back drummer who desires to
take a long term session approach with a new project, and
build my music up to performance level.

If you're interested, or you would like more info, feel free to
holler back at me. Thanks.

CH

Reply: William Wyndell . . .

Dear Caldwell: I got your response and I looked at your website, you big dork. But I can look past all of that. The music is simple, but I think if we speed it up just a tad, and work on a bad-ass stage show, complete with pyrotechnics and strippers, we could go places.

Look, I already told you...I have a kit and I am ready to fuckin' jam. I got a friend that plays the electric guitar and he might be interested. He's mostly into stuff like WASP, IRON MAIDEN, SLAYER, SATANS HELPERS, and SACRED EVIL, but he's looking for a change of pace, too. Let's rock.

Talk with you soon, asshole.

William

Reply: Caldwell Haine . . .

Heh, heh. The vision you paint reminds me of a KISS show I went to. Come to think of it, I even saw Maiden back in the day.

Well, I appreciate your enthusiasm. What you suggested for a stage show is not quite what I had envisioned. The p-technics could be useful in the future. The strippers get a thumbs down from me.

Thanks for your suggestion about the lead guitarist. I already have a lead person I work with. I want to stick with a 3-piece unit for starters and build a solid framework. It's easier to manage a smaller band.

Do you have some of your music that I could listen to? I'd like to hear some different styles and tempos. My music is more syncopated than most styles, so jazz and reggae chops will certainly help. Some of the drummers I like are Neil Peart, Stewart Copeland, Carter Beuford, and Buddy Rich.

CH

Reply: William Wyndell . . .

Look here, asshole, I could care less that you went to a KISS concert...big freakin' deal. Who hasn't seen KISS? Paul Stanley's chest hair makes my ass wet.

It's cool, we can keep it a 3-piece. I agree that smaller bands are easier, but you have to have good musicians to make the music feel and sound full. I KNOW I can pull my weight! Can you and that other buffoon you play with?

Neil Peart is my idol. I am also into Steve Gadd and Omar Hakim. Anyways, enough of that shit. When do you want to meet and jam? Also, what's with the "no strippers" comment? This isn't some sort of gay band is it? Nothing against fags, but I am not into gay bands.

Ok, let me know the info I need. Later, William

Reply: Caldwell Haine . . .

William, I am trying to keep an open mind about you, but your brash statements are making that very difficult. If you would like to talk more, I'm open to that. But I would appreciate you toning down your language and your delivery. Otherwise, best of luck to you.

Reply: William Wyndell . . .

Dude, why are you being such a pussy? Let's fucking jam.

To:	pianoron@earthlink.net
From:	William Wyndell
Subject:	*Piano Lessons*

Hi. I want to take keyboard/piano lessons. I know this might sound crazy, but I have a physical handicap. I only have one hand…the second just has a sort of round stump with a fingernail on the end of it. Will you still work with me?

Thanks. William

Reply: Ron D'Arcangio . . .

Hello, William.

I'd be more than glad to work with you. There is plenty you can do with one hand, and if you're interested in modern keyboard technology, there's a lot you can do with a fingernail.

I'm excited to see what we can do. My rates are $25 an hour in my home studio, or $35 for house calls. Let me know if you would like to set up some lessons. — Ron

Reply: William Wyndell . . .

Sounds super. Is there any sort of discount or 1/2-price rate since I have only one hand? Also, should I start growing that fingernail longer?

Reply: Ron D'Arcangio . . .

Unfortunately the rate is 'per hour' as opposed to 'per hand'. Otherwise I'd be glad to adjust it. As far as the fingernail goes, it just needs to be able to push a button. Is it your left or right

arm? If it's the left we can develop it to play basic bass lines.
Thanks. — Ron

To:	info@fxrock.com
From:	William Wyndell
Subject:	*New Band Member*

I read that you guys are looking for a drummer for your stupid
band. Look no further. I fucking jam hard, dude. I want to
play with ya'll. Let's freakin' rock the house down and see if we
can't make some people sick in the process.

I hope you dorks don't suck, 'cause I don't. I am the best, so
when we do gigs and get paid and we are dividing the money
up, I will require a little bit more than the rest of you guys.
And if you or anyone else complains, I will beat the shit out of
you. Are we clear? Hurry back.

Have a good day.

William Wyndell

Reply: fox rox . . .

Alright, you got yourself an audition. Tell me what times you're
free this weekend…Saturday, Sunday afternoon would be
good, or whatever. We'll see if you are the best, and if you're
not, we'll break your elbows for wasting our precious time. Oh,
we'll do it.

Chris — 555-4806

Reply: William Wyndell . . .

Don't worry about my playing, Sporto...you and the rest of those yahoos you play with better be practiced up and ready for me. Tell me when and where and I'll see you there.

Are we going to change the name of our band? Our name sucks. I have many great suggestions. Hurry back, son.

William

Reply: fox rox . . .

Saturday afternoon, around 2 P.M., Francisco Studios #2. Look for a sign on the door saying ROCK (on the first floor).

The name stays, Holmes. But your name, we may have to do something about that. I'm thinking 'Pierre'. I'll see what the others think about it.

Reply: William Wyndell . . .

Hey, homie...sorry for the delay. I got arrested for kicking my girlfriend's ass (the bitch) and just got out of the pokie.

I know where Francisco Studios is...I used to rehearse up on the 3rd floor. How about this coming Saturday? Let me know.

Reply: fox rox . . .

Are you available at all this week or weekend? We anxiously await the arrival of the new drummer and your spunk seems to be the only think missing from this band. If you could e-mail your phone number so that we may easily contact you, that would be a big help.

Patrick

Reply: William Wyndell . . .

I just sent an e-mail to that other address. You guys got a website or some band photos you can e-mail? Hurry back.

William

Reply: fox rox . . .

Not really, www.foxrox.com will give you an idea of what our mp3's sound like. Let's work out something this week so that we can jam Friday or Saturday.

Reply: William Wyndell . . .

Hey there, pal. I went to your website and listened to a few "hot licks". Man, you guys suck shit…and your old drummer sucked worse than the rest of you bozos.

So I have decided that if I am to join, I will require 60% of our net intake at the door. That is good with me and very fair. Saturday is good. What time? Hurry back, son.

William

Reply: fox rox . . .

Saturday isn't going to work for us. How long have you been playing the drums? And what kind of kit do you have? Is it going to break all the time like our old drummer's? Do you have decent cymbals?

Reply: William Wyndell . . .

Oh yeah, so what about Sunday? You think any of those other dickheads have plans or can we jam?

Reply: fox rox . . .

You are something else, man. Sunday is good. It's gotta be in the early afternoon, around 3:00 P.M. is perfect. We're not heavy metal and we don't beat up our girlfriends. Do you know where to meet us?

Reply: William Wyndell . . .

Quit being a dork, dude. Yes, I know where Francisco Studios is. Maybe one of you assholes can meet me on the side of the building so I will know who the hell you guys are. Hurry back, and don't make me wait.

Reply: fox rox . . .

#2 is in a corner to the left of the McKinney entrance. Have you been in any bands? What names were they?

Reply: William Wyndell . . .

Yep, been in lots of bands and ALL of them TONS better than this one. Room #2...I know where it is.

Reply: fox rox . . .

Do you REMEMBER any of the fucking names??????

Reply: William Wyndell . . .

Yeah, I remember all their names but it's none of your business.
I am going to bed, asshole. I'll see you on Sunday.

Reply: William Wyndell . . .

Look here stupid...I am getting e-mails from two sides over
there. Do you want me in your retarded band or what? Since
Sunday is no good for someone, then Monday is good with
me. Let me know.

Reply: fox rox . . .

Sunday is good. I am sure Monday won't be good for us.
Sunday at 3 P.M. A phone number would help so we can call
you to hound your ass so that you show up this time.

Reply: William Wyndell . . .

Hey retard, last time we didn't have anything set in stone like
this time. I'll be there at 3 P.M. I like to smoke lots of pot...is
it cool to burn doobies in the band room?

You can't have my number because I don't know you yet, so
quit asking...don't EVER ask me again for my
number...EVER. Are we clear?

Reply: fox rox . . .

Well, we waited for you Sunday, and then left after that. We may be up there Monday or Tuesday. Just show up so we know you exist.

Reply: William Wyndell . . .

Maybe.

Reply: fox rox . . .

What a waste of time you are. Don't e-mail again.

Reply: William Wyndell . . .

So we gonna jam or what?

Reply: fox rox . . .

Patrick here…probably not, since you seem to leave us hanging all the fucking time. We can't call you to confirm anything, and you haven't shown up twice. We can't waste anymore time.

CHAPTER EIGHT

On How to Get a Job

To:	shadowrestaurant@hotmail.com
From:	William Wyndell
Subject:	*Restaurant Work*

Hello. I would like to work at your new restaurant. I have experience in serving, bartending, bussing, dishwashing, cooking, and eating. I live in the Heights so I am really close to the restaurant. I gladly accept any position, and seeing how I have done all the stupid jobs listed above, you can just put me wherever. It doesn't matter to me because I am a team player.

I guess all I need from you is my start date and what position I have (so I can dress appropriately). Thank you so much. I am looking forward to hearing from you.

William Wyndell

Reply: Shadow restaurant . . .

William,

Can you come in for an interview this week or next? We would like to meet you. Please call me at 555-7500 to set up a time, or e-mail back a time that works well for you.

Thanks. C. Smith

Reply: William Wyndell . . .

Hello there, Ms. Smith.

Thanks for the e-mail. Yes, I accept the position. You are saying that you want me to start this week or next? Either is good with me. But, you didn't say which position you hired me for.

This is important so I can get my business cards ordered. Please let me know.

Sincerely, William Wyndell

Reply: Shadow restaurant . . .

William, please call me at 555-7500 to set up a time to come fill out an application and interview, or e-mail your resume.

Thanks, C. Smith & Mr. Steinwir

Reply: William Wyndell . . .

Hello Ms. Smith and Mr. Steinwir.

I got your e-mail. I already went ahead and ordered my business cards yesterday. I will pick them up on Monday. I wasn't really sure of our logo, so I just made one up.

Also, I wasn't sure which job you hired me for, so on the cards I listed Chef and Chief Waiter. Is there anything else I need to tell them before they print 500 cards? Also, I will start Wednesday. What time do you want me to be there? Looking forward to working for you.

Warmest regards, William

Reply: Shadow restaurant . . .

Sorry, William. Hope you can get a refund on the cards. We won't be needing you.

Reply: William Wyndell . . .

I don't understand. I have been a good employee. On what grounds am I being terminated?

To:	evolv99@hotmail.com
From:	William Wyndell
Subject:	*Event Promotions*

Hello Sir.

I saw your ad and see you need someone to promote events for you. That is what I do. My grandfather played violin in the symphony for nearly 46 years, and my grandmother owned a pet store. You can see that promoting events runs in my blood.

What kind of events will I be promoting? Let's get this ball rolling. I am happy to join the team.

Warm regards, William Wyndell

Reply: Jason Harringin . . .

Please call for more information.

Sincerely, Jason Harringin — 713-555-4514

Reply: William Wyndell . . .

Good morning, Jason.

Thank you for the quick reply. I went out to the garage and dusted off the tent that I have used for various promotional events. I need the name of our company so I can come over and set it up, give you a full demonstration, and then I can fill out my employee paperwork. Thursday is good with me, so hurry back and let's confirm. Thank you very much.

William

Reply: Jason Harringin . . .

Please call me so I can explain to you more about the company. Thanks.

Jason Harringin — 713-555-4514

Reply: William Wyndell . . .

Hi again, boss.

I am a bit confused. I thought you wanted me to come over and set up my tent and do a demonstration for you and the people in our office? What does that have to do with me calling you? As far as I know we were past all of that. So, I guess Thursday is still a go. I will mark it in my book as confirmed. If I am forgetting something to bring, let me know. Thanks a million.

William

Reply: Jason Harringin . . .

I think you are confusing me with someone else. We have not only never talked before, we definitely have no arrangement for you to come to our office and set up a tent. What are you talking about? Please call me so we can straighten this out ASAP.

Sincerely, Jason Herrington — 713-555-4514

Reply: William Wyndell . . .

Hello again, boss.

Why are you confused?

Back to business, I went and got the tent cleaned at one of those high-pressure water cleaning places, so it looks great. I am sensing you need more time to prepare, so I will do the demonstration on Friday instead of Thursday. Do I need to bring chairs for you and the audience or will you supply me with those?

Thanks in advance. William Wyndell

Reply: Jason Harringin . . .

Look, William, I have no idea who you are or what the heck you are talking about. You obviously have gotten my e-mail address confused with someone else's. If I was your boss, I'd probably know who the heck you were. I had an ad listed in the Houston Press that had the title of promotions, but we haven't even spoken about setting you up with an interview. If you're interested you can call me, but otherwise realize that I have nothing to do with you setting up some tent for whatever you are talking about. Please straighten out your information.

Thanks, Jason Harringin — 713-555-4514

Reply: William Wyndell . . .

Hello Mr. Harringin Sir.

What don't you understand? Now look, if you are not the person I need to set my tent up and do the demonstration for, then tell whoever that person is that I WILL be there Monday morning, April 12th, at 9:45 A.M. and to be there. I will be set up in the parking lot. It will be hard to miss me. The tent is about a 30' x 30', and the canopy has red and white stripes. If you still want to supply the chairs, then have him/her bring them. If not, let me know and I will bring my own. If you have any other questions, let me know. Sorry about all this confusion, but it's really not that difficult. Have a super day.

Regards, William Wyndell

Reply: Jason Harringin . . .

With the utmost respect I'd have to say that you are really one big dipshit. I've read all the stupid e-mails you've been sending an associate of mine as well. I guess you have nothing better to do than amuse us with your silly antics. You've given us some good laughs but I'd appreciate it if you'd quit e-mailing me and my other coworkers. Hope you find something to do with yourself. Heck, you're probably a 13-year-old kid just messing with people in your spare time between algebra homework and history assignments. Have a great day.

Jason Harringin

To:	jconsulting@aol.com
From:	William Wyndell
Subject:	*Jennings Consulting*

Dear Ms. Rogers:

I am applying for the entry-level marketing or promotions position you are seeking to fill. I will be a tremendous asset to your team.

I am not sure exactly what I will be promoting or marketing, but I'll promote the shit out of it. You can count on me to do whatever it takes to get those jerks to buy, buy, buy.

Your advertisement doesn't say how much you will be paying or anything about benefits. Would you explain in your response to me? Also, I will be starting next Monday. It is not important that you provide me with a company car at the beginning, but we can negotiate that next week. I know where the office is, so I'll see you on Monday.

I will await your immediate response with further instructions, and look forward to my first day of work.

Sincerely, William Wyndell

Reply: jconsulting@aol.com . . .

William…I appreciate the humor of your letter. However, I need you to submit a resume before "starting your first day of work on Monday". I will need your resume before I go in to any details about the company. As for the company car…what you drive is your company car!

Thanks, Ashlee — Jennings Consulting

Reply: William Wyndell . . .

Dear Ashlee:

I don't know what you found to be so funny. If you are making fun of me in some sort of way, that is very unprofessional of you. But maybe you are new, so I can understand.

As far as a resume, why do you need a resume at this point in the process? I already said that I accepted the job. As far as I am concerned, it is set in stone. Let's not make this any harder than it is. Now, I am somewhat of a claustrophobic, so my office must either be next to a window, or near an open area (maybe by the water fountain area). I understand about the company car. I will just use mine for now. Will I be receiving a per diem for gasoline for the daily commute? Please advise.

I look forward to meeting you in person. I will see you next week.

Kindest regards, William Wyndell

Reply: jconsulting@aol.com . . .

William:

Unless advised by me that you have been asked BY ME to come in for a preliminary interview, you do not have a job here, nor do you hold any position whatsoever. I was in no way making fun of you, simply complimenting you on your approach to inquiring about the position.

As I said before, unless you somehow managed to send a resume, came in for an interview with my manager, and got hired without my knowing…you do not hold a position here.

Send ME a resume…through fax or e-mail…and we will go from there. If not, then please stop wasting my time. I have several other people who are serious about this position, and I am very busy dealing with them.

Thanks so much. Ashlee

Reply: William Wyndell . . .

Dear you:

This is total bullshit. I am not understanding why you are treating me like this. Do you treat all the other employees at the office like this, or just me?

If you cannot accommodate my specifics for my office area, we can talk about it. But you don't have to be rude and mean to me. So is Monday still a go with you? Let me know. Thanks so much.

William

Reply: jconsulting@aol.com . . .

Obviously you are not, and cannot, be serious. Here is a number to call and discuss any further questions you may have: 555-2006. You may ask for Ashlee. Thank YOU so much.

Ashlee

Reply: William Wyndell . . .

Dear Ms. Ashlee:

Are you aware of the Equal Opportunities Act? This clearly states that I am entitled to all the rights forwarded to me as an employee of your company. Now, since I have not gotten all the specifics about my first day, I think it is fair to inform you that I will now be starting work on Wednesday instead of Monday.

Also, could you tell me exactly what department I am to report to? I would prefer something in Sales or Marketing.

Thanks so much, Ashlee. — William

To:	j&d@mail.ev1.net
From:	William Wyndell
Subject:	*J&D Marketing*

Hi. I am looking for a job with J&D Marketing. I understand this is a good job for a college student. So…what do you want me to market?

In conclusion, I will accept the job. I also conclude that we will need to talk about this further...end of conclusion.

Conclusively yours, William Wyndell

Reply: j&d@mail.ev1.net ...

William,

I like your style—sometime being a maverick is good. Are you money-motivated? I am going to cut out a lot of steps and cut to the chase. Call my cell, 555-0047. If I'm tied up, leave a message and I'll call right back. Play your cards right and you will have $200-$500 in your pocket this time next week.

Jimmy

To:	michellehr@yahoo.com
From:	William Wyndell
Subject:	*Restaurant Manager Found*

Good morning, Ms. Shimmel.

I am e-mailing you about the advertisement you placed for the Manager position. I will be a huge asset to your team.

I have 10 years of restaurant management experience. The restaurant I recently managed was just shut down by the health department for being dirty, so now I am seeking employment with you.
Before I start, we need to clarify a few issues. I must have a moderately high salary and full benefits. A company cell phone and laptop computer is not a must at first, but eventually I will

need these items. I am willing to work ALL national holidays, including Thanksgiving, Christmas and Easter. But I must have off every July 17th and October 5th. My religion doesn't allow me to work, eat, drink, fornicate, or talk to people on those particular days.

I have one final question: Will I receive any type of "signing bonus", and if so how much?

In conclusion, it looks like everything is a GO on this end. When I start, is there a particular uniform I must wear, or is business casual fine? Please let me know before I show up wearing the wrong thing on my first day of work. I look forward to being a member of your team. See you next week.

Sincerely, William Wyndell

Reply: Michelle Shimmel . . .

Hello. My name is Michelle Shimmel and I have received an e-mail from you. I have yet to receive your resume, so I am unable to discuss any opportunities that may be available for you. If you would like to be considered for any job opportunity, send a resume (either fax or e-mail). If you meet the qualifications, we can set up a phone interview.

Thank you, Michelle — (888) 555-6473

Reply: William Wyndell . . .

Dear Ms. Shimmel.

Or is it Mrs.? I don't think you and I are on the same page. I already said that I accepted the job and listed my additional requirements for employment. So I am not understanding all of this "run-around" that you are giving me.

Are you aware of the Equal Opportunities Act? This clearly states that you cannot fire me for my religious beliefs, sexual orientation, or any government affiliation. Do you understand firing me for any of these puts you in violation of the law?

I will speak to you about this on my first day of work.

Sincerely, William Wyndell

Reply: Michelle Shimmel . . .

Mr. Wyndell, we are definitely not on the same page. I am not sure who you think I am. I am a recruiter with Manage Recruiting and I work with numerous restaurants in staffing their managers. I wish you success with your new position, but I am not the person to contact about your dress code, days off, or anything else you require.

Best wishes, M. Shimmel

Reply: William Wyndell . . .

Dear Mrs. Shimmel:

You need to quit passing the buck and blaming others for your incompetence as a recruiter. I am willing to forget about all the anguish you have caused me thus far, but further legal action on my part will greatly depend on where you place me for work.

Secondly, you will have to increase my salary by 1%. I will expect this done. Please respond immediately.

Thank you. William Wyndell

CHAPTER NINE

On Banking

To:	info@centrbank.com
From:	William Wyndell
Subject:	*Account Information*

Dear bank:

I am new to the area and am interested in opening an account over there at your place there. I have only about $24.86 at the moment. I do professional rodeo, got gored by a bull, so I am not doing any riding presently. So I was wondering if you have some sort of program where I can borrow some more money and put it in my new account with you. Also, what is the penalty for writing them hot checks?

Please let me know so I can start my new account with you.

Sincerely, William Wyndell

Reply: info@centrbank.com . . .

Mr. Wyndell,

The minimum opening deposit for our Central Free Checking is $50.00. The fee for Non-Sufficient items presented to the bank is $23.00 per item. I cannot answer your question regarding the loan you are seeking due to a lack of information. You will need to visit one of our banking centers and speak to the lending officer at that location, or you could call them and discuss the loan over the phone with them.

Thank you for your inquiry regarding the bank. I hope the information above has been helpful.

Reply: William Wyndell . . .

Thanks for the reply, that's super. $13.00 is pretty cheap for me writing all them hot checks. So, it looks like I will use your bank. Here is my Social #. . .it's 464-89-9976, and I want them numbers put on them checks.

I will worry about the loan later. I just found some money yesterday so I might be good for another couple of weeks. So it looks like I will be using your bank there. That's super. So you going to send me them checks or do I need to come on over there and get them? And when can I start writing them?

Hurry back. William Wyndell

Reply: info@centrbank.com . . .

Mr. Wyndell,

In order to open an account with us you will need to visit one of the banking centers, present two forms of identification (one with photo identification). You will need to make a minimum deposit of $50.00, and you will also need to qualify. Checks will be ordered at the time the account is opened. I do want to restate that the fee for a non-sufficient check is $23.00 for each item.

All the details and options on the account type that you select will be reviewed with you at the time you open the account.

Reply: William Wyndell . . .

Dear Mr. Info:

Once again, I appreciate your reply. That's just super. Does it matter the two forms of ID's that I bring? One is my Texas license, but when I got my most recent DWI, they cut the picture off . . . said it was suspended or something…I don't know, I wasn't really listening, so I forgot. But I do got one of them Malibu Grand Prix licenses and it has my picture on it. It is ok?

So it is $23.00 when I write one of them hot checks? When did it go up from $13.00? Also, please tell me before I come if it is necessary to bring any of my school, dental or police records or anything like that. Ok then, that's super…just super.

Thanks a million. William

Reply: info@centrbank.com . . .

Mr. Wyndell,

No, the two forms of identification you stated in your previous e-mail are not acceptable. Central Bank cannot open an account for you, nor can we order any checks for you.

We appreciate your inquiry. However, we cannot serve as the bank to meet your financial needs. Good luck in hunting for a bank, and goodbye.

CHAPTER TEN

On Movies and Theaters

To:	046@cinema.com
From:	William Wyndell
Subject:	*Theater Complaints*

Dear Sirs:

I have a few concerns about your movie theater that I wish to address to you, and I will expect your immediate response before I spend one more dime there. Many times while I am watching a movie, there are people who rudely chat on the telephone with their friends. This has happened on at least 14 recent occasions. When this happens, am I entitled to a refund? Or, will I be kicked out of the theater if I start a fight with that particular person?

Secondly, I would like to ask that you stop showing "Horror" movies. They give me nightmares and are not good for me.

Thirdly, the price of your Twizzlers is too high. If I pay $3.50 per bag and I eat 10 Twizzlers, that comes to about $.35 per Twizzler. I have tried to return the excess Twizzlers in my bag to the counter for a refund, but the Manager said it was not possible. Could you explain to me why I am not entitled to a refund?

And finally, I would like to be selected to vote for the nominees and winners of the various awards shows. If I can look past all of your movie theater's inadequacies, can you guarantee me a position working with the Academy?

Thank you for your time. I will look forward to your immediate feedback. Happy viewing.

Sincerely, William Wyndell

Reply: 046 Rose . . .

Mr. Wyndell,

I don't want you to become entangled in any confrontation for
people talking on their phones during the movie. We have signs
and slides placed throughout the theatre explaining we do not
tolerate phones during the showing. I assure you the ushers are up
to checking out the theaters to prevent interruptions during your
or anyone's viewing. This is the first time I have heard any com-
plaints on this issue being at this theatre. I have had problems at
other locations, and have dealt with them with some success.

As for the Horror films, they are booked through Corporate,
and I don't think this will change. They are a big draw for the
various patrons that come to the theatre.

As for the high price of the Twizzlers, I will make a mention to the Head of Concession in the Corporate Office. However, the last price increase was put in effect after a recent market survey of our competitors, and the pricing decisions were based on their findings.

Thanks. Don Barrings

Reply: William Wyndell . . .

Dear Mr. Barrings,

I cannot make promises, but I will do my best to refrain from using excessive violence towards patrons who talk on their phones while I am trying to enjoy my movie.

Now, do you have any connections with the people at the Academy? Can you help me? — William

---

To:	koening@beanstk.net
From:	William Wyndell
Subject:	*Movie Theater Rep.*

Dear Sir:

I would like to speak to you about the Marketing Rep position. I will be a tremendous asset to you in many ways.

I understand I will be selling advertising and trivia for the Meyerland movie screens. This is great, as I am a huge movie fan and critic, so I know our target audiences. Plus, as an added bonus for hiring me, I can write the trivia questions for the audiences. My friends say I am a real "Cliff Klavin" when it comes to bits of worthless trivia. For example…Did you know the Kimono dragon only urinates once every 2 weeks, and it's enough to fill up 4 one-gallon containers? See, not too many people know that.

Also, am I to understand that I will be working only for commissions? That is fine but would you please explain the commission structure in further detail? Are there any benefits?

I look forward to your reply. I am happy to begin a new career with you. By the way, what is the name of my new company?

Sincerely yours, William Wyndell

Reply: koening@beanstk.net . . .

Please take a look at www.cine.com/rep.html, then give me a call on Tuesday and set up a time we can meet. 555-5112.

Thanks. David Koening
VP Sales & Marketing — Screen Advertising, Inc.

Reply: William Wyndell . . .

Hey there, Boss:

Everything looks great on this end, so I am assuming we are a "Go". But you have failed to describe my salary and commission structure. I hope that since I am new to the company, you won't continue to blow me off when I request information. Please let me know. Also…what am I suppose to wear to work?

Thanks a bunch. William

Reply: koening@beanstk.net . . .

Dear William,

If you had read the page I sent to you, you would have seen: "Independent Marketing Reps are paid 15% commission on advertising sold and are paid monthly after the completed order, artwork and deposit are received".

I have a full schedule of candidates to interview today, but if I don't find one acceptable, I'll call you to schedule an interview later in the week.

Frankly, I was offended by the tone of today's e-mail message.

FYI: Our on screen trivia program features interesting facts about movies and movie stars. It would be offensive to the audience to pose a question about the pissing habits of the Kimono dragon

Reply: William Wyndell . . .

Hey, Boss.

Well, I went and checked out the website again. Looks good. It is acceptable to me, so I will still work for you.

So, you can go ahead and do your little stupid interviews today, but I can assure you that you won't find anybody can sell stuff like me. I am the best. Let me know when you want me to come up there and start.

Look forward to hearing from you, Boss. Take care.

William Wyndell

To:	rob@landmark.com
From:	William Wyndell
Subject:	*Movie Theatre Manager*

Hello. I am interested in speaking to you about the Manager position at your theater. I have six years of theater management experience at Cineplex theaters in Austin.

I am a huge fan of independent and foreign films. At my last theater of employment, I was known as "The Enforcer"...I threw people out on their asses when they chatted on their cellphones during the showings. So, we will have no problems there.

In conclusion, it looks like I got the experience, the know-how, and the brawn to fill this position. I live just around the corner, so I will never be late, and can work 7 days per week. Do I need to fill out anything before beginning work, or should I just show up and start?

I will await your response with further instructions. Thanks so much, Robert.

Sincerely, William Wyndell

Reply: Robert Arcain . . .

I apologize for the delay in response, but our initial ad gave us a swamp of applicants, and filtering through them has been exhausting. I am sorry to say that the position has been filled. Thanks for your patience.

Robert Arcain

CHAPTER ELEVEN

On Medical Research and Studies

To:	B.shaw@tmc.edu
From:	William Wyndell
Subject:	*Child Study*

Dear Mr. Shaw.

I would like to volunteer my child for inclusion in your study on children with learning disabilities. I think he would be a good candidate. We have never taken him to a therapist or doctor in the past. Me and my wife just assumed he was just sort of dumb…maybe it was something he inherited from my wife, because she's not the sharpest nail in the box (if you know what I mean). But maybe now we are thinking it could be more.

What steps do we need to take in order to place our son in your study? I look forward to hearing from you.

Regards, William Wyndell

Reply: B.shaw@tmc.edu . . .

Dear Mr. Wyndell,

Thank you for taking the time to write to me about your son. We are studying brain development and functioning in school-age children, and are comparing test and MRI scan results from kids who do and do not have autism to look for systematic differences. From the sound of things, your son might be eligible, but I couldn't be sure without interviewing you further.

Most of the slots we have left are for kids with pretty severe problems, but that does not mean that we can rule out your son's participation based on what you've told me.

Call me at 555-2580 and I'll be happy to talk more with you about our research, and to interview you briefly to try to figure out if your son is a match for our project.

Sincerely, Bill Shaw — Project Coordinator

Reply: William Wyndell . . .

Hello, and thanks for the reply. I hope our boy, Chet, can be in your study. I must tell you that when he was about seven months old, the housekeeper dropped him on his head. We had him wear a football helmet for four years after that...just to be safe. But I don't think that has anything to do with him being a stupid ass. Like I said, I think it is the genes he inherited from my idiotic wife.

Is the study done at the medical center? I work nearby. Would you like me to bring Chet over for an interview so you can get a better understanding of his abilities, or lack-thereof? Please let me know.

Regards, William

Reply: B.shaw@tmc.edu . . .

Dear Mr. Wyndell,

We have to exclude children with a history of significant head trauma from the study. Head injuries can easily cause unusual brain development, and adding children with brain trauma to our study would introduce sources of error. He may qualify for future studies. If you remain interested, please call me and I will be happy to add your child's information to our database.

Sincerely, Bill Shaw

Reply: William Wyndell . . .

Hello. I am sorry that you can't use Chet in your study, but I understand. I have another idea, though. Would it be possible that we do the study on my wife? I have already told you how she isn't the brightest star in the sky...as a matter of fact, she is downright moronic. I married her partly because I felt sorry for her for being so stupid, and partly because she had an incredible body. Let me know and we can come over any time that is good for you. Talk to you soon.

William

To:	info@allergyresearch.com
From:	William Wyndell
Subject:	*Allergy Study*

Hello there. My name is William and I want to be a subject in your study. I am 33-years-old and have all the symptoms you describe, including sneezing, runny nose, itchy nose, and nasal congestion. My eyes get so puffy sometimes that I look like the Elephant Man punched me in the face.

I have been allergic to ragweeds for well over two years...more like five years or so. Sometimes it makes me break out in a rash. I currently have one on my arm, and another in my genital area. However, I think the genital rash is some sort of STD that I got last month in Thailand.

What is the next step, and when can I start? I look forward to hearing from you. Have a wonderful day.

Sincerely, William Wyndell

Reply: Patty Mendez . . .

Mr. Wyndell,

Thank you for your inquiry. Please accept my apologies for not receiving my earlier reply. I e-mailed you prior to say based on study-specific criteria, we would not be able to ask you to come in for a screening. Good luck in getting your allergies tested.

Regards, Patty Mendez

To: dr.mori@utmb.edu
From: William Wyndell
Subject: *Depression Study*

My name is William and I want to take part in your study for depressed people. I can't seem to get out of the rut I've been in for the past two years. And I don't know if it's because I am stupid or because nobody likes me and I can't do anything right...or because I am not very attractive and I'm not good at anything, and I also hate my job...and I'm stupid.

Would I be getting some help should I be picked for your study? Let me know.

William

Reply: Mori, Blanche C (Psych) . . .

William—

The purpose of this study is to investigate and to evaluate the antidepressant efficacy of a new investigational drug versus placebo in outpatients diagnosed with Major Depressive Disorder (MDD).

You will be reimbursed $35 per visit for each that you attend at the end of the study. All the study medication and study-related procedures are at no cost to you.

Attached you will find a few questionnaires you can fill out and e-mail back to me. If you have any questions, do not hesitate to call me toll free at 1-866-555-MOOD.

Kind regards, Blanche Mori — Clinical Research Coordinator

Reply: William Wyndell . . .

Hello, Ms. Mori.

I was beginning to think you forgot about me like everyone else does. Everyone forgets about me because I am no good at anything. I really want to be a part of your study, but don't understand all that "medical talk" you used in your e-mail. I know that I am stupid and maybe that's why I can't understand anything...ever...because I am stupid and hate myself for being so stupid and ugly.

May I be in your study? I must know if you guys plan on doing hurtful things to me, like shocking me or hitting me while I am heavily medicated. This won't happen, will it?

Thanks. William

Reply: Mori, Blanche C (Psych) . . .

William,

In our studies, we do not shock or hit our patients. We do everything possible to make your appointments as enjoyable as possible. The studies involve medication and questionnaires. I can call you if you give me your number, or you can call me.

Kind regards, Blanche Mori

CHAPTER TWELVE

On Trading

To:	lazybonz@earthlink.net
From:	William Wyndell
Subject:	*Campaign Buttons*

Dear you:

I read your ad and understand that you are looking for old campaign buttons, posters, ribbons, and what-nots. I have a huge collection of that junk that was given to me when my mother passed away. She was an avid collector or worthless stuff like that. I personally collect important things, like firearms and explosives.

Now back to the matter at hand. I have buttons for almost all Presidents and Presidential nominees, including Governors and Senators for the past 50 years or more. I have 2 huge boxes full. I even got Wallace buttons, God rest his good, God-fearing, Klan soul.

So, are you interested in them? Are you looking to buy, or are you looking for a handout? I would be more than happy to trade you for something. What do you have?

Regards, William Wyndell

Reply: Joe Ginger . . .

William, William, William.

Yes, indeed I am interested in the very fine "junk" your mother collected. I am looking to buy, of course! I will always trade, too. I don't have any firearms, but I have just picked up some kind of fraternal sword in the original scabbard, if that counts. I might be willing to trade for that if there are any buttons of value in the group.

As in all collectable fields, there are "rare" items, and those that are common as dirt. Most groups include 95% common stuff and if we are lucky there may be a "goodie" or two in the bunch.

Now, how to go about this? Send photos via e-mail? Or send photocopies via snail mail? If I see what you have I can make an offer in cash dollars, or dinars, or something.

I am looking forward to hearing from you. Thanks again for writing.

Sincerely, Joe Ginger

Reply: William Wyndell . . .

I am glad you are interested in all this stuff. Were you dropped on your head when you were a baby or something? There is WAY too much of this stupid crap for me to take pictures of every little single thing. I told you I have two giant boxes of it (thousands of items). Why don't you tell me a rarity or two and I will look for them. Or, you could come over here and go through it all, but if I catch you stealing anything, I am going to take it out of your ass.

As far as trading, that sword sounds like a doozie. If the blade is big enough, I might can use it on a pig hunt, and stab it in the heart. I would be interested in any sort of weapon you might have for trade. I am also interested in any old dirty mags or '80's porn that you might have boxed up.

Let me know what you think. I will be away for three days at a Klan rally, but will e-mail you as soon as I get back. Take care.

William

Reply: Joe Ginger . . .

Well, are you local? I live outside of Athens, Georgia, and I'd be glad to come and look at it all. I probably was dropped on my head at one time or another. I might have some older "dirty" mags somewhere, too. You know how it is with us collectors…can't throw ANYTHING away! No, I don't steal. Okay…later is fine.

Have fun at the rally!

Reply: William Wyndell . . .

I'm back, Joe.

The rally was a complete success. We burned several crosses, and then protested all those pinkos in the government that are now allowing them men queers to have butt-sex with each other. It is a disgrace and a hard blow to the South. We will rally again next weekend. Don't worry my friend…the South will rise again!!

I live in Texas, so you will have to tell me what it is you want and I will look. Either that or you will be driving your ass off to look at all this stupid stuff.

What kind of porn you got for me? I am really fond of anything with John Holmes, Seka…and if you have AssBlasters VI or VII, then we for sure have a deal. Hurry back.

William

Reply: Joe Ginger . . .

I can't imagine you wanting to go through all those things to search for something you don't have any idea about. I'll go out in the building today and see what I have in the way of vintage porn. I can scan the covers and send you pictures if you like.

Here's another thing I collect…images of vintage nudes from the Internet…heh heh heh.

Reply: William Wyndell . . .

Hey Joe…man, you really are a pervert. Hell, at least my porn is modern. Why the hell you want to see a bunch of old, hairy ladies with FUPA anyway?

The Wrath of William Wyndell   **123**

I did a quick look around...I found some "I like Ike" buttons and a "Democrats for Ike" . . . also there are some Huey Long buttons and stickers, and some "Honkeys for Huey" . . . lot's of goodies here. So you want all this shit or what?

Ok, I will give you all this stupid crap in exchange for your medieval sword (for pig hunting), your porn collection, and $197 so I can pay my parole officer this month. What do you think?

William

Reply: Joe Ginger . . .

Well, when the photos were taken they weren't old and hairy... just young and frisky. I dunno...that seems like a lot of $$ for a "pig in a poke" or "stupid crap".

I would probably take a chance on it all for around $100, plus I pay postage, and include all the old porn that I have stashed. I still have to go out there and see what porn is still there. How does that sound to you?

Reply: William Wyndell . . .

You just let me know when you got all the goodies and get back with me. All right? Hurry up, stupid.

William

Reply: Joe Ginger . . .

Hey there, William. I went out there and tried to find my "stash" of mags. This is what I found. There may be more out there somewhere, and a couple of others that have more damage to them. Any interest in these?

I am about to go out of town for a week or so. I will leave on Tuesday. Hope to hear from you before then. — Joe

Reply: William Wyndell . . .

Where the hell are you going anyway, ya stupid? You got some sort of NAMBLA convention or something?

Reply: Joe Ginger . . .

Deal's off.

CHAPTER THIRTEEN

On Pets

To:	rollo33@yahoo.com
From:	William Wyndell
Subject:	*House for Rent*

Hello, Rolando. I am interested in renting a house from you. I am interested in most any place that you have, but I must have a backyard, and a big one if possible (for my "pet"). Please let me know what you have.

Thanks so much. William Wyndell

Reply: Rolando Sanchez Jr. . . .

Thank you for your e-mail. What kind of pet do you have, and what weight range or species? I may be reached by my cell phone and can answer some of your questions. 555-6799, in 512 area code.

Thank you for your time and attention. Rollo

Reply: William Wyndell . . .

Hi, Rollo...how's it going? I have a small horse...he's one of those mini-horses, kind of like a midget, but a horse. Do you have a house that has a yard for him? I promise, he doesn't make ANY sound at all. Please let me know.

William

Reply: Rolando Sanchez Jr. . . .

I need to talk with my brokers. Can you keep him in the Austin city limits? Or, do you need a place out of town? I will speak next with the brokers on Monday.

Rollo

Reply: William Wyndell . . .

Hello, Rollo. Yes, he can stay in the city limits. He likes the city. I told you, he is a mini-horse and he is very small.

Last year I kept him inside my apartment. I could still keep him there, but he was kind of hinting around that he wanted a yard to run around in. So please keep me posted.

Regards, William

Reply: Rolando Sanchez Jr. . . .

Hello, spoke with my broker... she would like you to contact us by phone. Our office # is 555-0099. We are here Monday through Friday 9:30 A.M. to 3P.M.

Thanks.

Reply: William Wyndell . . .

Hi, Rollo. Unfortunately I cannot call you. The horse ate my phone over the weekend and it will probably be another few weeks before I have time to get another one. What about if we just pick a property with a yard...I'll bring the horse and let him run around and see if he likes it...then we can go from there. Sound good? Let me know.

William

Reply: Rolando Sanchez Jr. . . .

I have been taken off the case. You MUST contact the office and speak with NANCY. She is one of the brokers. YOU must speak with HER.

555-0099.

Reply: William Wyndell . . .

Does she like horses? She sounds like a horse hater.

I still don't have a new phone but I need to move pretty soon. This stupid horse is starting to eat everything in my apartment. He needs a yard. Where do you want us to move, and when?

William

Reply: Martin Properties . . .

Got the info from the city on what is required to keep a miniature horse on our property. Is your horse a female or a gelding? Please give me a call, so we can meet at the property (with your horse).

We will be off quite a bit during the holidays, so call me ASAP if you want the house. My phone is number 555-0099, or you can leave a message at 555-1233 (AFTER 3 P.M.).

Thanks, Nancy Lemmi — Leasing Manager

Reply: William Wyndell . . .

Hi, Nancy. Thanks for the e-mails. Do you like horses? I was under the impression from Rollo that you were a horse-hater. Anyways, the horse is a male...he is fixed, so no worries there. I would like to move next week. As I told Rollo, I don't have a phone to call you. The horse ate it about 10 days ago. What is the address of my new house? Thanks so much.

William

Reply: Martin Properties . . .

Hi William...

I like horses...I was just not sure if they were legal in the city. You will have to build another fence...horses are required to be a certain distance from the neighboring houses, and this has to be done prior to moving in with the horse.

The address is 107 Richcreek, and it is $675 per month. Call me from a payphone to make an appointment to see it (and for me to meet the horse). Office 555-0099, cell 555-1233. I will be busy this weekend, so call me today. We need to get started on this right away since we will only be in Monday and Tuesday next week, and we will have to process your application (and with the holidays, it could take longer with people being off).

Thanks, Nancy

Reply: William Wyndell . . .

Hey there, Nancy...How's it going? Sorry it has taken so long to get back with you. I have been away for the holidays. I put the horse in the car and went on vacation...took him to DisneyLand, the Grand Canyon, and Roswell, New Mexico. He likes to look for aliens and alien spacecraft.

So, everything is looking great...the house is perfect, I will build another fence, and everything looks just dandy. You didn't give me a move-in date. Since it is the weekend, I will start packing today and will drive all my stuff over there on Wednesday. I will also put the horse in the yard starting Tuesday evening. Thank you.

William

E-mails from Hell

Reply: Martin Properties . . .

William,

Nancy isn't due back till Monday, but I was checking messages and thought I should point out some things. The house on Richcreek currently has a lease pending on it, though I don't know yet whether or not Nancy has approved them or not. Also, have you ever set up an appointment for Nancy or Rollo to show you the house or for Nancy to meet the horse? I know that she likes to meet all pets over 15 lbs to get a feel for them.

Last of all, have you ever turned in an application with us? We do need to put all potential tenants through an approval process.

Please get back to us as soon as possible. Nancy should be in the office tomorrow and I would advise you to get in touch with her as soon as possible.

Stephen — Martin Properties

Reply: William Wyndell . . .

Hi, Stephen,

Do you like horses? I know that Nancy says she likes horses, but I don't think she does...I think maybe she is a horse-hater, so I didn't know if it was a company policy for all the employees to be horse-haters or not.

As far as I know, I had been talking to Rollo, and I was assuming everything was a GO. I have discussed the move with the horse and he is really excited about it.

So...it looks like we got the horse, the house, and are now

waiting on Rollo and Nancy to put the final stamp on things. When is the move in date? Thank you.

William

Reply: Martin Properties . . .

I'm afraid the other potential tenants have been approved. I'm sorry you couldn't get back to us in time, and I'm afraid Nancy told me that we don't have any other properties well-suited for a horse. The backyard at Richcreek is pretty unusual.

If you have any questions, please give Nancy a call at 555-0099 between 9 A.M.-3 P.M.

Sincerely,

Stephen — Martin Properties

Reply: William Wyndell . . .

Hi, Stephen.

I am sensing that I didn't get the property because the people at your office are horse-haters? Is this so? Not letting me move into that house, as promised, because you don't like horses is a form of discrimination. Are you aware of the Discriminatory Act of 1982?

Reply: Martin Properties . . .

William,

You did not get approved because you never gave us an application. The people that did get approved submitted an application and an application fee. They did these things before you even confirmed that you even wanted to live at Richcreek. Nancy asked you to call her to discuss this, but you never did.

Last of all, pets are not a protected class in Austin. It would have been interesting to have a property with a horse, but you wouldn't even give us a chance to meet it. By the way, were you aware that miniature horses aren't allowed to live in apartments in the Austin city limits? Their enclosure has to be at least 10 feet from the nearest neighbor.

Sorry we couldn't have been more help,

Stephen — Martin Properties

Reply: William Wyndell . . .

So you are saying I can't move in anymore? Is it because you don't like horses?

Reply: Martin Properties . . .

Answer to question #1...Yes. Answer to question #2...If you had submitted an application and a deposit that we could verify, you probably would have gotten the place. The horse had nothing to do with it.

To:	emathew0@hotmail.com
From:	William Wyndell
Subject:	*Dragon*

Hi. I read your ad and see that you are selling a dragon. Really . . . a dragon? I have never had one, but I think it would be a cool pet. I don't know a lot about them or how to care for them. Do I need to buy some sort of cage that is fireproof, so when it breathes it won't burn my house down? Please let me know.

Thanks a lot. William Wyndell

Reply: Eric Mathews . . .

I must have been sleeping when I typed this. It is a bearded dragon…a lizard…and doesn't get much bigger than a foot. I'm asking $175ish for the whole set up. Let me know what you think.

Eric

Reply: William Wyndell . . .

I am a bit confused. Does the dragon breathe fire or does it not breathe fire?

Reply: Eric Mathews . . .

It's a "bearded dragon". A lizard. Do you really think anything is capable of breathing fire?

Reply: William Wyndell . . .

Hi Eric,

I have seen many movies with fire-breathing dragons and if you read any folklore, it will describe fire-breathing dragons in detail. So this dragon has a beard and does NOT breathe fire? Is that a fair assessment?

Reply: Eric Mathews . . .

Actually, the dragon does breathe fire. First it was the walls of the living room, then the carpet, and now the house. When it sneezes there is fire...when it sighs there is fire...when it pants there is fire. Hopefully it will fire your computer...then you won't be able to e-mail me.

To:	dcCatz@mail.com
From:	William Wyndell
Subject:	*Kittens for Sale*

Good morning.

I am inquiring about the 3-month-old black kittens you are selling. I would like them. I need them for my show. How many of them do you have that I can buy right now?

Also, when will you have more? I will have a show with "Steve" once per month, and we will need 3 or 4 kittens each time. Is this a problem?

Please advise as soon as you can. Thanks a bundle. — William

Reply: DC . . .

Hello. Please tell me more about your show and what the kittens will be doing in it. Also, let me know what kind of animals you already have and what kind of home you will be giving the kittens.

Thanks.

Reply: William Wyndell . . .

Hey there, DC. I can answer a couple of questions pretty easily. The kittens will be used in a show I do with my pet snake "Steve". We do it once a month at a bar...it's called "Feeding Frenzy Friday"...and we usually feed the snake small rats and birds. We will start this month with kittens.

When can I buy them, and how many do you have? Let's get this transaction going. Hurry back.

Regards, William (and Steve)

Reply: William Wyndell . . .

I haven't heard back from you. Are you offended or something? You're not one of these "hug a tree" people are you? If you are having any doubts, just think about it as Alfred Einstein's theory of Survival of the Fittest. It is a natural occurrence. Hurry back now.

William

Reply: DC . . .

I e-mailed you last week…twice. I asked you to please tell me about the home you will give the kittens and the "show" you are talking about. Are you looking for a pet or a side show act?

Your e-mails are very strange, do not make any sense, and you are very impatient. You will need to answer my questions, or stop e-mailing me.

FACTS: ALBERT EINSTEIN, not Alfred. And Survival of the Fittest is Charles Darwin, not Einstein. Do your homework.

Reply: William Wyndell . . .

Hello, DC. Thanks for correcting my Einstein facts. You seem smart. What are you, some sort of botanist or something?

Okay…I thought I answered your questions sufficiently, but I will do it again in case you are a bit slower than most people. Currently I have a pet snake, iguana, and newt. I take my snake to the club and people pay a cover charge and watch me feed him (Steve) various animals.

Regarding the kittens, they will be in a home filled with love. My daughter loves kittens, so she will love and play with the kittens everyday. She already has names picked out for them. They will stay at our home until it is their time to be taken to the club, at which time they will be chased around the cage by Steve. Once he catches them, he terminates them by squeezing them to death…then he will eat them whole.

That's basically it in a nutshell. When can I pick up the kittens? Hurry back.

William (and a hungry Steve)

Reply: DC . . .

Don't ever e-mail me again.

CHAPTER FOURTEEN

On Shopping

To:	mach1@hotmail.com
From:	William Wyndell
Subject:	*Mustang for Sale*

Hi. I'm inquiring about the '71 Mustang you are selling. You say it has a 351 V8 engine?

Currently I am driving an old souped up El Camino. Will the Mustang be much faster? Also, I need to know if the cigarette lighter works. If I am to drive the 'Stang, I have to make sure I am able to smoke for the "cool looking guy" effect. Let me know.

William Wyndell

Reply: Bill Branden . . .

William…Sorry it has taken so long to get back to you. It all works, and is an awesome car…FAST. Give me a call if you want…555-3838.

Bill

Reply: William Wyndell . . .

Hello, Bill.

Everything sounds good. I have 3 requests:

1. Would you be willing to buy me a cover for it? I am afraid if I am to park it under the tree in my yard, there will be too much bird shit hitting it.

2. Would you be willing to make a copy of all the tapes you own so I can listen to them while I'm driving the 'Stang?

3. Would you be willing to throw in a few movie passes for me and my honey? If so, how about some vouchers for free popcorn and Twizzlers?

If you can say "yes" to at least two of my requests, I can say "yes" to buying your car today. Let me know.

William

Reply: Bill Branden . . .

As long as this is no joke I can work with you. Are you aware what I am asking for it? Please give me a call. We can set up a meeting. You need to see the car.

Bill

Reply: William Wyndell . . .

Hey, Bill.

I don't have a phone. I have heard that they can cause cancer to the ear, so I don't use them. I don't use Sweet & Low either.

I think I would be willing to forfeit my request for the tapes, and probably even the car cover. Instead, I read that Disney on Ice is coming to Houston and I would like to go. How about a few tickets to that? All in all, I think this is going to work if, like I said earlier, you can meet my demands.

When do you want to make the transaction? Let me know.

Reply: Bill Branden . . .

I am leaving today to go to Austin thru Sunday. How about we meet up the first of next week? You know we are asking 25K for it, right? If so, then let's talk some business.

You cannot be disappointed in the automobile. It's awesome. Try and give me a call if you can, otherwise let me know how to get in touch with you.

Reply: William Wyndell . . .

Hey there, Sport. I know I will not be disappointed in the 'Stang. What do you say there, Chief...we got us a deal? Can you meet my demands, especially the Disney on Ice tickets?

Let's meet next week. How about City Streets? I was there last week and got tossed out for pissing in the beer tub. Let me know.

Reply: Bill Branden . . .

Who is this? Give me your number.

Reply: William Wyndell . . .

What do you mean? This is William. I am hesitant to give my number out to strangers. When and where the hell you wanna meet me, Sporto? Hurry back.

Reply: Bill Branden . . .

Sorry—but these e-mails are pretty funny. Just making sure this is not a joke. I can meet you anytime this week. The West Alabama Icehouse is a good place. It's outside so you can take a good look at the car. But you need to give me your number, or call me so we can set it up. Have a good one.

Reply: William Wyndell . . .

Alright there, Champ…I know where the Icehouse is located. I got arrested there one time for selling pot. I was supposed to go down to Vidor (TX) this week for a rally. Seems that now we got these men queers trying to pass laws that say they can marry each other or some shit like that. How about later this weekend…does that work for you, Sport?

Reply: Bill Branden . . .

I am probably going out of town on Friday. But, I'll be back late that night.

Reply: William Wyndell . . .

Where the hell do you think you are going? This is bullshit.
Why the run around all of a sudden?

Reply: Bill Branden . . .

Look, pal, I will be at the Icehouse Saturday evening about 7 or
8 P.M. with the car. If you want to see it, go there. I do not
need this runaround from you—you are one strange dude. If
you want to seriously buy this thing, be there on Saturday.
Otherwise, forget it.

Reply: William Wyndell . . .

Hey there slick…now don't go tootin' your horn at me. YOU
are the one that was giving ME the runaround. If I show up are
you going to have those Disney on Ice tickets or what? Hurry
back, son.

Reply: Bill Branden . . .

I was there with the car on Saturday — missed you. A lady
there wants to buy it for $25,500. Can you beat that?

Reply: William Wyndell . . .

I sure can…How does $25,600 grab ya?

Reply: Bill Branden . . .

Alright look, we need to speak on the phone and meet. Otherwise I am just wasting my time. Call me as soon as possible.

I am leaving for New York on Sunday (thru Tuesday). So call me before then or after, but if we don't get something set up by the end of next week, I am going to go ahead and sell it to that lady.

Bill

Reply: William Wyndell . . .

Why the hell are you going to New York? See, now I am getting the runaround again. This is total bullshit. Why do you keep giving me the shaft? All I want to do is buy your cockadoodie car.

Reply: Bill Branden . . .

Listen, William. I am through messing around with this. I have given you plenty of opportunities to come buy it. I will sell it to you tomorrow (Friday) for $25,600 and that is it...no tickets...no run around...no bullshit.

You have my number. I suggest you call me and we can set this up for tomorrow or I am selling it to the other lady.

I don't want any comments, either. Just tell me you will come to the Icehouse and at what time and we will do the deal, have a beer, and you can drive the hell out of it.

Bill

Reply: William Wyndell . . .

Hey, hey, hey…don't get your panties in a wad. I was just tired of you giving me the shaft. You mean you will not throw in the Disney on Ice tickets? Okay then, what about the movie tickets?

Reply: Bill Branden . . .

I will be back from NY on Tuesday. If you want to buy the car you WILL call me by Wednesday. Otherwise that is it. I am done with this e-mail account.

Bill

Reply: William Wyndell . . .

Hey there, Phil.

Is that with or without the Disney tickets? Please advise.

William

Reply: Bill Branden . . .

Last chance. Had an offer for $25,900, told the guy it was a deal come Wednesday the 15th. Let me know by then. No tickets, just the car. I will give you one chance…Cashiers Check before Wednesday. You have to call though.

Reply: William Wyndell . . .

Sorry there, Phil…no Disney tickets, no sale.

Reply: Bill Branden . . .

Do yourself a favor in the future, amigo—don't waste people's time. I have absolutely no need for the bullshit you dished out over the last month. Take your shit somewhere else, I don't need it.

Get a job, get a hobby, or get a life, I don't really care, but definitely don't get pissed at me for the fact that you can't handle an easy business deal like a respectable person.

To:	akeel12@yahoo.com
From:	William Wyndell
Subject:	*Barbie Dolls*

Howdy there, Ma'am. I seen your ad and seen you're selling them Barbie dolls. I was wondering if you had any of them dolls that wet themself, just like a real-life baby. I like them dolls a lot. How much you charging for them?

Regards, William

Reply: akeel12@yahoo.com . . .

Dear Wyndy Willy-less, Thank you for your inquiry. Get a life. My Barbie's are probably worth more than your double wide, you loser.

P.S Check your Depends diapers if you need something that wets itself. Thanks.

To:	article@yahoo.com
From:	William Wyndell
Subject:	*Chainsaw for Sale*

Hello there, sonny. I saw your ad and see you have an electric Remington chainsaw for sale. I need one.

I live just north of Buda and broke my last one slaughtering a horse for a family bbq. I am not all familiar with electric saws…will that cut through bone and fur? Please advise.

William Wyndell

Reply: article@yahoo.com . . .

FUCK YOU, BIG TIME! HOPE YOU DIE SO THE WORLD CAN BREATHE EASIER.

Reply: William Wyndell . . .

Hey there, sonny…why all the hostility? I am guessing it WON'T cut through bone and fur? Hurry back.

William

Reply: article@yahoo.com . . .

HOPE YOUR NUTS TURN INTO THE SIZE OF A
SESAME SEED, THEN DROP OFF. IF I SAW YOU I'D
BUST YOUR FUCKIN' JAW.

Reply: William Wyndell . . .

Why all the hostility? Are you one of those "save the seals" kind
of people? Why don't you sell me the chainsaw? And why all
the filthy language?

Reply: article@yahoo.com . . .

FUCK YOU, ASSHOLE.

To:	rashmi@hotmail.com
From:	William Wyndell
Subject:	*Bed and Trundle*

Hey, top of the mornin' to ya. I am interested in your dumb
little bed and trundle you are selling. Your ad doesn't list a
price. I will expect you to hurry up and get back to me with a
price so I can start laying down on the god-damned thing.

Have a nice day. William Wyndell

Reply: rashmi kali . . .

Ooh lala...William Wyndell wants a 'trundle'! The price for the bundle is $1350. Will it hurt Will's bills????

Cheers, Rashmi

P.S...Specs for the offer include the following..........(don't waste your precious time on collecting and tailoring the accessories...its all added here in this comfy and gorgeous bed...!!!!!!!....BTW, its fresh/rarely used.....proof enclosed:)

- "Pottery Barn" daybed with trundle
- "Simmons Beauty Rest" twin mattress set
- tailor-made cushions—4 pieces per daybed from "Sunbrella"
- mattress pad and comforters made from white goose-down (hypoallergenic)
- custom-made back rest with covering
- mattress coverings

Note: the pillows and bed covering are no-stain and non-fade fabric. Don't do a dumb thing by loosing it...hurry up.......!

Reply: William Wyndell . . .

Wow, Rashmi, you must be a pole smoker. I don't know any guys that know that much about beds and bedding. A little "light in the loafers"? Am I right or am I right?
It sure is a lovely set and I am sure I will pull all sorts of ass on it. The price may be a bit high. Can we meet somewhere a tad lower? I hope so...I really want that god-damned bed.

Hurry up and respond. William

Reply: rashmi kali . . .

William,

We could offer this to you at a minimum price of 1200 bucks. Please let me know if it suits you!

Best, Mrs. Rashmi Kali

Reply: William Wyndell . . .

Hey there, and top of the mornin' to you, Klauson. Sorry, I wasn't able to get online yesterday. I was having some differences with my fucking boss. Now look here, al Jazeera, your price sure seems high. How about something around $1050? Say it is so and I will come get it today. Will that work? Again, I will expect you to get back to me immediately.

Thank you, William

Reply: rashmi kali . . .

$1200 is the best price. I have moved from $1500 to $1200 (original price was over $2300).

Reply: William Wyndell . . .

Hey, Ramullah,

That bed WAS worth $2300, but that was before you and that spouse of yours got on it and got it all greasy, dirty and stinky.

So, how about $1150? Again, I will expect you to drop everything that you are currently doing and get back with me IMMEDIATELY.

William

Reply: rashmi kali . . .

Okay. You can contact 555-0302.

Reply: William Wyndell . . .

Hey, stupid, I tried to call you last night, but nobody answered. I hope 3 A.M. is not too late to be calling. When can I get that god-damned bed?

Reply: rashmi kali . . .

Call it again at an earthly hour! You can have it.

Reply: William Wyndell . . .

Hi again. Top of the mornin' to ya, Raji. I called you again last night, but I waited until 5 A.M. Why weren't you up? How much sleep do you need, lazy ass? Hurry back. I want to lay on the trundle.

William

Reply: rashmi kali . . .

Call between 8:30 A.M. to 10 P.M.

Thanks.

Reply: William Wyndell . . .

I cannot call you during that time as I am at work. I do not finish work until 11:30 P.M. Should I call at midnight?

Thank you.

Reply: rashmi kali . . .

I don't want to go back and forth over e-mails. As you told me, I dropped everything urgent and attended your mails. So, please act fast if you really want it.

Bye.

Reply: William Wyndell . . .

Hey there, Kasbah...I looked up your address in the phone book and drove over there last night. It was about 12:30 A.M. or so. I was outside honking. Why didn't you come outside? I had money in-hand and was ready to make the deal. Hurry back.

William

Reply: rashmi kali . . .

Sorry you can't do this until we have an arrangement! This sounds crazy as any unknown person can honk outside our door! Please don't indulge in any such act unless we have spoken. Kindly call ASAP and fix a good timing. We shall be then glad to go ahead.

Please call now!!!! — Cheers.

Reply: William Wyndell . . .

Hey there, Akbar. I thought you said you wanted me to come over again and honk? I was out there last night honking for about 15 minutes, or for at least enough time for me to drink 3 beers, and you never came out. I could hear a dog barking...was that yours or the neighbor's? Ok, I will be out there again tonight. See you then.

William

Reply: rashmi kali . . .

Sorry, we cannot meet you until you call.

Bye

Reply: William Wyndell . . .

Good morning, Haji. Well, tried to call you several times...I think your wife answered but I didn't feel like speaking with her, so I hung up on all occasions.

I am coming over at midnight on Sunday to pick up that bed. Now, I found a formula to calculate the value of used beds and trundles. In order for me to up my giving price of $1300 I must know the following:

1. How many meals were eaten on it?

2. How many times did you and your wife have sex on it? Was it over 80?

3. How many times did the cat or dog either piss or shit on it?

I will expect you to answer my e-mail at your highest priority level, and I will see you at midnight sharp!

Warm regards. William

Reply: rashmi kali . . .

Sorry, we cannot meet you until you call.

Reply: William Wyndell . . .

Hello again, Ghandi. I didn't hear back from you...what's your problem? Unless I hear back from you IMMEDIATELY, I will be at your house at 12:30 A.M. sharp...I'll be in a Ryder truck outside honking. See you then, al-Zawahiri. Have a nice day.

William

Reply: rashmi kali . . .

Which address? What are you talking about??? There is no address by my name in any place. Stop wasting your time...

Reply: William Wyndell . . .

I was there last night. It wasn't at 12:30 like I said. I was a bit late because I had gotten into a fistfight earlier that night. However, I was out front at 3:45 A.M. and was honking, and you never came out. Now, since we had an agreement and a meeting and you never showed up with that damn bed and trundle, I will expect a reimbursement of $117.89 for the rental of the Ryder truck. If you decide you will not sell me the bed, I will come get the cash from you on Tuesday morning. Hurry back, Remshi. — William

Reply: rashmi kali . . .

Shut-the-fuck-up or this al-Jazeera will get your mommy
screwed by Bin Laden's dog rite in her ass hole!

Reply: William Wyndell . . .

Hello, Rashmi.

Are you aware that making terrorist threats puts you in violation of the U.S. National Security Act of 1989, article
a.41.g.12, and subjects you to termination of your green card?

You are hereby served and notified that you must report to the
local Immigration Office immediately. Failure to appear will
result in termination of your green card, incarceration, and
fines not to exceed $35,000. If you have any questions, please
let me know IMMEDIATELY, or we will expect your presence
on Monday, April 5 at 8:30 A.M. If you cannot afford an
attorney, one will be provided.

Regretfully, William Wyndell

Reply: rashmi kali . . .

The bed is sold. Stop e-mailing me.

Dear you:

I am e-mailing in regards to your ad about the stuff you have for sale: 6-burner oven, mosaic tiles, floor tile, counter tile, and antique parlor stove.

Now look…I don't need all that shit, so why are you listing it? All I want is the 6-burner oven. So subtract all that other stupid shit off your $4,300 price and I think we can make this happen. Do you hear me, son?

Get back with me pronto. I'm hungry and I need that stupid oven.

William Wyndell

Reply: Andrew Dowell . . .

You can take the Southbend for $450. Just the parlor stove is $4300. Give a call, and lighten up. You don't need to be rude over a little miscommunication.

Andrew
555-8614

CHAPTER FIFTEEN

On Potpourri

Hello.

My name is William and I am new to Houston and new to the St. Michelle's Catholic Community. I am very interested in joining the church's Young Adults Club.

I wanted to see what was on the upcoming agenda, and when and where the group meets? Also, if you ever need some help in planning or organizing fun things to do, I would be more than happy to help. I would like to see more nights during the week of heavy alcohol drinking, and maybe we could take the group to Louisiana to go gambling. It doesn't really get any better than a good night of drinking and gambling. It is paradise.

Anyway, sorry to ramble on. I really look forward to joining the club. I will await your e-mail to let me know about the above.

Thanks so much. William Wyndell

Reply: Martha L. Mars . . .

William,

Thanks for your interest in the Young Adults Club. I will be glad to assist you, but do you have the calendar on e-mail? If you forward me your mailing address, I will get a May calendar in the mail to you immediately. I will also include a membership application.

Thanks, Martha Mars — Recording Secretary

Reply: William Wyndell . . .

Hello, Martha.

I have just a few questions that maybe you can help me with:

1. When is the first drinking party?

2. How much are dues?

3. Will there be any sort of "probationary" period, like there was when I pledged my fraternity? If so, is there any hazing involved?

4. At the next drinking party, are there many single chicks?

I have to get back to work. Please e-mail me as soon as you can with answers to my questions.

Thanks again. William

Reply: Martha L. Mars . . .

William,

You have some misconceptions about our group.

Q1—We have Thirsty Thursday each month sponsored by one of our officers at Las Alamedas. We also have Happy Hour scheduled sporadically throughout the year.

Q2—Dues for Singles is $5.00 per quarter the 1st year, and $20.00 due January 1 for every year after.

Q3—The purpose of our group is to establish an atmosphere of Christian ideals. We have religious, cultural, recreational, and social activities to bring about a personal bond of Christian charity. Upholding these ideals is essential to maintaining membership. There is no probationary period or hazing.

Q4—I cannot answer your question regarding single women, as we do not release the personal information of any of our members.

As I mentioned in my previous e-mail, if you would like a calendar, please send me your mailing address. We would be glad to include you in our June newsletter.

Thanks. Martha Mars

To:	wade@burrito007.com
From:	William Wyndell
Subject:	*Burrito Accident*

Dear Sir and Ma'am:

My name is William Wyndell. I recently ate at your restaurant. At first, my wife and I thought it was a good dinner. We both had the burrito…she had chicken, mine was beef.

After several hours we were both feeling a bit queasy. Before long we both had a severe case of diarrhea. Normally I wouldn't care, but since we were on the road, we had problems.

First of all, the diarrhea and pain never stopped for 2 hours. My wife had an accident in the front seat of our car. I made it to the nearest gas station. However, I didn't make it to the toilet, so my Dockers got soiled and ruined. As for her pants, they too were ruined, and she left a stain in the front seat of our car.

We are e-mailing in hopes that you will pay for our cleaning bill to get the diarrhea off the car seat, and also for two pairs of ruined pants. We are willing to overlook all the pain, suffering, embarrassment, and anguish from the severe cases of diarrhea your food gave us. She wanted to ask for more because most women don't like the feeling of pissing out of their ass.

I will await your immediate response and attention to this matter.

Sincerely, William Wyndell

Reply: Wade Beamack . . .

Mr. Wyndell—

Thank you for taking the time to give me your feedback. As I am sure you can understand, I have to report all claims of customer accidents to my insurance carrier. I would be more than happy to file a report, however I will have to get the following information:

- Date of your visit
- Time of your visit (exact time)
- Appropriate time of sickness
- Ingredients made in your burrito
- Your wife's name, address, and phone number

If you would like to forward me a phone number, I would be more than happy to contact you.

Regards, Wade Beamack — President

Reply: William Wyndell . . .

Dear Mr. Beamack:

I appreciate your expedient response. That is very professional of you. However, I am not understanding nor liking all this "runaround" you are giving me.

My wife's name is Beatrice and she feels the same as I in that all we want is our stuff cleaned and/or replaced. What do you want...a picture of the diarrhea all over the car seat? Would it make you happy to see pictures of piss exploding from my ass? Is that what we have to do?

Look, I don't know WHAT was in the burrito. It was all just

regular stuff like lettuce, tomato, onion, cilantro, the habanera sauce, etc. But, whatever was in there completely tore the ass out of us.

Regards, William

Reply: Wade Beamack . . .

William—

Your response is unprofessional, as well as offensive and disgusting. If you would like to make a claim, it will be handled by my insurance company. If you forward all the information I requested, I will have them contact you.

Wade

To:	elsam@hum.org
From:	William Wyndell
Subject:	*Africa Volunteer*

Good morning. I am interested in speaking to you about doing some volunteer work over in Africa. I am a schoolteacher by trade, and I read that you need people to go over there and train teachers. That is what I would like to do.

I have a few questions that hopefully you can answer:

1. Will it be possible to ever ride an elephant or zebra?

2. Would I be allowed to bring any firearms for hunting? I collect elephant tusks and although illegal, I would like a few more.

3. What is the youngest legal age should I choose to bring a bride back to America from Africa?

I look forward to your immediate response to my inquiries. Hopefully I can get there soon and start teaching and training the people who greatly could use my help.

Kindest regards, William Wyndell

Reply: elsam@hum.org . . .

Hello William—

I think maybe you have applied to the wrong organization. Why don't you join a Safari Team and go hunting for both deer and wife?

Regards, Else Marto

Reply: William Wyndell . . .

Sounds great. How big are the deer in Africa?

To: rollsroyce@yahoo.com
From: William Wyndell
Subject: *Fashion Industry*

Hello, Ma'am:

I read your recent internet ad and see that you are seeking employment. I must say I am impressed with your credentials. I understand you are looking to either stay in the fashion industry or are looking for a way into the fashion industry.

I think I have something that will be right up your alley, and may be the next closest thing to a fashion career proper. Are you familiar with aluminum siding? The possibilities are endless. E-mail me back at your earliest convenience and I will explain your new job further.

Kindest regards, William Wyndell

Reply: Danyeal Owann . . .

Hello. You have my attention..............please tell me more.

Thanks!

Reply: William Wyndell . . .

Hi, Danyeal:

I am glad that I have your attention, as I very well should. I didn't understand if your ad said that you were currently IN the fashion industry or that you WANTED IN. If it is the latter, then I feel that getting into aluminum siding first will help you reach your goal.

The pay is incredible, and the work is not only fascinating, but rewarding. I would like to know a little more about your work history before we go any further.

I look forward to hearing from you, Danyeal. Have a wonderful day.

William Wyndell

Reply: Danyeal Owann . . .

Hello.

My desire is to enter the fashion industry. My background has been as a financial analyst with a mortgage company for 5 years, and with the voting solutions industry for 8 months. I have a Bachelor's Degree in Finance, and I am looking to change the direction of my career.

Tell me more about this business opportunity.

Reply: William Wyndell . . .

I am impressed. With your degree and experience in finance, and your desire to enter the fashion industry, I think aluminum siding will be a perfect fit for you.

I am looking to bring someone in here in short order, and I think you just might have what it takes to succeed in the aluminum siding industry. Aluminum siding will be the fastest step you can take to get into the fashion industry. Aluminum siding can best be described in two words: fascinating and amazing.

In addition, we offer full benefits. When is a good time for you to come in and fill out your paperwork?

Thanks so much, William Wyndell

Reply: Danyeal Owann . . .

What position will I be interviewing for? What is the name of your company, and where are you located?

Reply: William Wyndell . . .

Hi, Danyeal. How are you?

I am happy to hear that you are interested in the position I am offering. Your official title (on your business card) will read:

Danyeal Owann
Aluminum Siding / Fashion Merchandising Coordinator

We have two offices…one in Austin, and one in Houston. I will be gone most of the day tomorrow. I think we will have to shoot for you coming to see me on Tuesday.

Also, do you know anything about ballbearings or Velcro?

Looking forward to meeting with you.

William Wyndell

Reply: Danyeal Owann . . .

What exactly does this position consist of? How exactly do fashion and aluminum siding coincide?

Reply: William Wyndell . . .

What do fashion and aluminum siding have in common?

Everything. It is really obvious if you think about it.
Your position will deal with ALL aspects of aluminum siding, as well as fashion merchandising and coordination. With your Finance Degree you will excel when called on to perform basic mathematical logarithms or dabble with long division and fractions.

Which day this week would you like to come in, talk, and fill out your paperwork?

William Wyndell

Reply: Danyeal Owann . . .

Where are you located? I am currently working a temporary job in Addison, so I can come in on my lunch hour if it is not too far. What is the name of you company again?

Reply: William Wyndell . . .

We are located over here in Cut and Shoot, so it shouldn't take you that long to get here from Addison. What kind of temporary work are you doing? I am sure you will be happy once you start here and begin working full-time again.

The name of your new company is TexAmerica Aluminum Siding and Fashion Merchandising. We currently employ about 100 people statewide. As per your request, I am going to pencil you in on Wednesday at 2:30 P.M. I look forward to meeting you in person, Danyeal.

Thank you, William Wyndell

Reply: William Wyndell . . .

Hi, Danyeal.

I haven't heard back from you and I need to make sure we are still on for Wednesday. I am NOT a mind reader, so I will need your confirmation for our meeting. Do you understand this order?

William Wyndell

Reply: Danyeal Owann . . .

I hope you get this message. I've been having problems with my computer. I can only assume you didn't get my message yesterday. Anyway, I won't be able to meet with you. My lunch hour is from 12:00 P.M. to 1:00 P.M.. I cannot leave at 2:30 P.M.

Reply: William Wyndell . . .

Dear Ms. Owann:

Received your e-mail, but it was a little too late. I thought you said you wanted to come at 2:30 P.M.? I blocked off a whole afternoon of my schedule for you. Why does it matter about your lunch from 12:00-1:00 P.M.? You are quitting your Addison job anyway and coming to join us.

I can look past this first delinquency without any punishment. From now on however, it would behoove you to listen to my commands and heed my orders. Are we clear?

With that behind us, how about we shoot for Friday? Anytime is good, so I will pencil you in for noon. See you then.

William

Reply: Danyeal Owann . . .

I will not be quitting my current assignment to come and work for your company. I also will not be meeting with you tomorrow. I am no longer interested in your open position.

Reply: William Wyndell . . .

Are you aware that we have already made space for you at our office? Did you or did you not say that you wanted to get into the fashion industry? You agreed learning the ropes of Aluminum siding was the best way to get in. So what is the problem?

Your current job is only temporary. It is imperative that you begin here next Wednesday. Do you understand this command?

Thank you, William Wyndell

Reply: Danyeal Owann . . .

I don't know you or anything about your company. I will not be coming to work for you next Wednesday or any other time. This will be my last e-mail to you. — William Wyndell

www.EmailsfromHell.com

www.EmailsfromHell.com